WHO'D WANT TO BE A COMPANY DIRECTOR?

A Guide to the Enforcement of Irish Company Law

Who'd Want to be a Company Director?

A GUIDE TO THE ENFORCEMENT OF IRISH COMPANY LAW

Mark O'Connell

FOREWORD BY

MICHAEL McDOWELL, TD

Published in 2003 by
First Law Limited
Merchant's Court,
Merchants Quay,
Dublin 8,
Ireland.
www.firstlaw.ie

Typeset by Gough Typesetting Services, Dublin.

ISBN 1-904480-08-X

A catalogue record for this book
is available from the British Library.

Printed by Johnswood Press Ltd

For my parents,
Joe and Teresa O'Connell

Foreword

I am honoured that Mark O'Connell has asked me to write the foreword for his work. His stated aim is to provide a guide for lay readers and, in particular, company directors as to their legal obligations, duties, pitfalls, and the penalties and liabilities which attach to those obligations and duties.

In my view, such a published guide is of great benefit for those who become involved with the management and direction of limited liability companies. Since they will be presumed in law to be aware of their responsibilities and liabilities, it is only right that they should have access to concise, readable texts in which those matters are outlined for them. Obviously a book of this size cannot deal with company law in all of its complexity. There are lengthy texts which deal with the more complex aspects of company law. And there are lawyers who earn their living from interpreting and applying the company law in its full complexity. The author acknowledges that a guide such as this aimed primarily at company directors and written in layman's language, is no substitute for sound professional legal advice.

There are good reasons for limited liability as provided by our company law. Incorporated companies provide continuity in the affairs of businesses which would otherwise be thrown into crisis by, say, the death of their owners. Limited liability companies also provide an orderly basis for investors to assist in the development of companies without exposing other assets in the event of commercial failure. Limited liability also acknowledges that there will be inevitable casualties in an economy in which enterprises are encouraged; in which they compete with each other, and in which strong enterprises are encouraged to prosper at the expense of weak and poorly managed enterprises. Commercial failure is an inevitability – not evidence of some moral deficiency. In a dynamic, changing economy, the reality of commercial failure has to be provided for, and dealt with, by a system of law which is fair to investors, employees, creditors and debtors alike.

Compliance with, and enforcement of, company law is generally speaking conducive to the effective and sound management of commercial activity in any society. A company which cannot manage its own affairs in a compliant manner is highly unlikely to possess many of the ingredients needed for sustained commercial success. While compliance is obviously not a sufficient condition for commercial success, it is a *necessary* condition.

Because Ireland needs to be an enterprising society, and because Ireland cannot be a caring society in modern conditions *unless* it is enterprising, it is of the utmost importance that high standards of enforcement and compliance should underpin the operation of limited liability companies in the State. The Office of Director of Corporate Enforcement and the Company Law Review Group which are now established on a statutory basis are two pillars of a new approach to corporate culture in Ireland. I was privileged to have a role in the evolution of those two institutions and of the Company Law Enforcement Act of 2001. I believe that they all contribute to a healthy corporate climate in Ireland and that they do not stultify or retard genuine, sustainable economic enterprise in any way.

I congratulate Mark O'Connell on his lucid exposition in layman language of the duties of company officers. His keen legal mind now devoted to his profession as a barrister is greatly complemented by his lucid style perfected during his very successful years as a professional writer commenting on the political and economic affairs of our State.

Michael McDowell, T.D.
August, 2003

Preface

Until recent times, the phrase "corporate law enforcement" was a favourite oxymoron circulating among lawyers and business people. Despite the existence of the Companies Acts – which proscribed over 120 acts and omissions in different areas of commercial activity – people running small and large companies in many cases quite simply disregarded the legal obligations which bear upon the operation of business enterprises. Those who enjoyed the privileges of being a director of an incorporated business did not appear to be aware of the duties they had. And if they did know about their responsibilities, there was a general feeling abroad that they didn't really have to fulfil them.

Part of the difficulty was that the regulatory authorities didn't exist in the same number and fashion as they do nowadays. If the owner of a small petrol station-cum-public house in Poulamucka never got around to filing his annual returns to the Companies Registration Office (CRO), he might get a letter two years later. He would pass the letter on to his accountant who would more than likely tell him not to worry.

Another problem related to the attitude of successive governments which – because unemployment was chronically high – treated employers with kid gloves. No minister wanted to stand in the way of an entrepreneur, someone who was going to provide jobs for people who would otherwise be numbered among the social welfare class or indeed join the Irish Diaspora.

As the economy improved from the early 1990s, the attitude towards defaulters – whether they be tax cheats or people who disregarded their obligations under the Companies Acts – began to change. In parallel with the strengthening of the sense of economic self-confidence grew an intolerance of those who flouted the law.

There was a political response too. In 1998, the government asked Michael McDowell, SC, to chair the Working Group on Company Law Enforcement and Compliance. A number of problems were identified ranging from lack of compliance, institutional weakness and the cowardly attitude of the political establishment. The proposals put forward by McDowell's group led to the enactment of the Company Law Enforcement Act 2001 which represented the first earnest attempt by any government to enforce the laws which had been in place since 1963 and before. The chief feature of the new legislation was the establishment of the Office of the Director of Corporate Enforcement (ODCE).

There are two parts to the role of the ODCE. As the title of the office implies, its principal duty is to secure the implementation of the Companies Acts so that business in Ireland can be carried on responsibly and efficiently. Along with the CRO – with which it has a strong working relationship – the ODCE has uncovered suspected breaches of the Companies Acts and has secured compliance in a variety of ways, including criminal convictions.

The second part of its role – and it is complementary to the first one – is to encourage greater compliance. The experience of the last two years has shown that the attempt to secure legal observance has been more than just a euphemism for institutional bullying. The publication of a series of seven information leaflets and consultation papers along with the ongoing seminars and presentations to bodies representing business interests and the professions, is testimony to this.

The legislation is having an effect. Enforcement and compliance are difficult goals to achieve – particularly against a culture in which Irish companies were permitted to default in their obligations. Along with the establishment of the Criminal Assets Bureau and the strengthening of the powers of the Revenue Commissioners, it is a truism to say that conditions have changed completely. Progress is being made, but it is slow. Despite the transformation in the legislative and institutional environment, there is a lag in the attitudes and the behaviour of many people involved in business in this country.

This book is a guide to the legal obligations of company directors. It aims to set out the range of duties, pitfalls and penalties about which people involved in the operation of Irish companies should be aware. In effect, it is aimed principally at the lay reader, the company director, rather than at practitioners. Footnotes have been included to assist those readers who want more than just the basic information. It is the hope that readers will find that the book highlights the important issues in an intelligible manner. However, it should not be seen as a substitute for professional legal advice.

Readers should also be aware of the Companies (Auditing and Accounting) Bill 2003 which is due to be enacted before the end of this year. This is an important piece of legislation which will have further implications for company directors. The Bill – among other things – proposes to establish the Irish Auditing and Accounting Supervisory Authority, the regulatory agency for auditors and accountants.

The Bill has left this author in an unenviable position. It would be foolhardy to incorporate all of the Bill's provisions into the book because amendments may still be made. The legislature is being undermined by enough people in the media and other places already; it doesn't need me to join the queue. That said, I have given notice of some of the main changes which are being considered.

I would like to thank Bart Daly at First Law – more for his sense of calm than for the shrill e-mail messages reminding me of broken deadlines. I would like to acknowledge my thanks to Dublin accountant, Kieran Corrigan who suggested the need for the book to Bart Daly. The sponsorship of Pat Delaney, the Director of the Small Firms Association, is much appreciated. I am grateful to Thérèse Carrick who edited the book and to Caitríona Foley. I would also like to acknowledge some of my learned colleagues: Gráinne Clohessy, BL, for her advice and Patricia Dillon, SC, for her kind support. I am of course thankful to Michael McDowell, SC, for his generous Foreword and for the encouragement he has always given me. I would like to express my appreciation to Paul Appleby, the Director of Corporate Enforcement, and to his helpful colleagues, Ian Drennan and Dick O'Rafferty. The brothers O'Connell, Fionán and Stephen, played supporting roles as they always do. My gratitude is also owed to Diarmuid Ó Ceallaigh. Finally, I thank my fiancée, Róisín Ní Eadhra, who endured countless conversations on such cheerless conversation topics as directors' fiduciary duties and section 150 applications. Bart Daly doesn't know this but without her, I would have thrown in the towel long ago!

Mark O'Connell,
Law Library,
The Four Courts,
Dublin 7.
August 22, 2003

Table of Contents

Table of Cases

Table of Statues

Companies Act 1990—*contd.*

Table of Statutory Instruments

CHAPTER 1

Company Formation

A company is an independent legal entity, which is most frequently formed for the purpose of carrying out business activities. Its separate legal personality sets it apart from the people who own and run it. The company can purchase property, enter into legally binding contracts, initiate legal prosecutions and it can be sued.

COMPANY REGISTRATION

The Companies Registration Office (known as the CRO or the Registrar of Companies) is the State authority charged with the job of incorporating new companies and registering business names in Ireland. It also has the function of receiving and registering a range of other documents, which must be filed during the lifetime of a company. Furthermore, it is responsible for enforcing the requirements regarding the filing of documents and for providing information to the public.[1]

The operation of companies is governed by the Companies Acts 1963–2001 along with EU legislation.[2] At the time of

---

[1] Its address is Parnell House, 14 Parnell Square, Dublin 1. Tel: (01) 804 5200, www.cro.ie.

[2] The main pieces of domestic and EU legislation are as follows:
- Companies Act 1963.
- Companies (Amendment) Act 1977.
- Companies (Amendment) Act 1982.
- Companies (Amendment) Act 1983.
- Companies (Amendment) Act 1986.
- Companies (Amendment) Act 1990.
- Companies Act 1990.
- Companies (Amendment) Act 1999.
- Companies (Amendment) Act (No. 2) 1999.

writing, the Companies (Auditing and Accounting) Bill 2003 is before the Oireachtas and is expected to be enacted by the end of this year.[3] The CRO issues companies with a Certificate of Incorporation,[4] but beforehand it needs:

- Original signed copies of the Memorandum of Association and the Articles of Association, both of which must be printed in black ink on durable paper;[5]

- A statutory declaration by the company secretary, its first director or its solicitor that all the registration requirements have been fulfilled;

- A signed document, known as Form A1, which includes details of the company's full name, its registered address, the names, addresses and occupations of the directors and secretaries as well as a statement that it will, when registered, carry on lawful activity within the state. The name must not be offensive and it cannot already exist;

- A statement of the company's assets, liabilities and expenses to facilitate the calculation of stamp duty;

- Confirmation that the company will have at least one director residing in the State. Where this confirmation cannot be given, the company must hold a bond of €35,395[6]

- Company Law Enforcement Act 2001.
- European Communities (Companies: Group Accounts) Regulations 1992 (S.I. No. 201 of 1992).
- European Communities (Branch Disclosures) Regulations 1993 (S.I. No. 395 of 1993).
- European Communities (Accounts) Regulations (S.I. No. 396 of 1993).
- European Communities (Single Member Private Limited Companies) Regulations 1994 (S.I. No. 275 of 1994).

[3] For more on this legislation, see chaps.5 and 6 on *Directors' Duties* and *Auditors*.

[4] S.6 of the Companies (Amendment) Act 1983.

[5] For more on the Memorandum and Articles, see below at pp.6 and 127–166.

[6] S.43(3) of the Companies (Amendment) (No.2) Act 1999.

as provision for penalties, which might be imposed in the event of the company being in breach of tax or companies legislation.

Once the Certificate of Incorporation is granted, a notice must be published in *Iris Oifigiúil*.[7] This is akin to a public declaration and gives legal security to shareholders and others dealing with the company. At this stage, the company has a legal personality of its own and can begin to trade.

Alternatively, companies many be pre-incorporated by company formation agents who sell them off the shelf to members of the public.

A company, which seeks to trade without satisfying the above requirements or before it receives its Certificate of Incorporation, is committing a criminal offence and is liable to prosecution.

In the first instance, efforts will be made to encourage such companies to remedy breaches. But if these fail, prosecutions will follow. Depending on the seriousness of the behaviour, the directors of the company who are found guilty on indictment can potentially be fined as much as €12,700 and/or be imprisoned for up to five years. If convicted summarily, the penalty can be as high as €1,900 and/or 12 months in jail. If the Court forms the view that the company has been trading fraudulently, it can impose a fine of €63,000 and/or a jail sentence of up to seven years on those directors who are deemed to have been responsible for the breach.

DIFFERENT TYPES OF REGISTERED COMPANIES

There are different types of registered companies. Depending on their size, purpose and physical location, registered

---

[7] *Iris Oifigiúil* is a gazette of approximately four pages, which is published twice each week by Government Publications. It contains information on a range of issues such as economic and commercial matters.

companies can be limited or unlimited, private or public. They can comprise just one person, they can be guarantee companies or they can be publicly limited.

Limited Company

Under the Companies Act 1963, a company can have its liability registered as limited because it affords its members personal indemnity in the event of the business not succeeding. The liability of the individual members is determined by the level of unpaid debt in relation to the share capital held.

Unlimited Company

The liability of the members of such companies is unlimited. It is common for creditors of companies to engage the services of a liquidator in order to get their debts repaid. The disadvantages must be considered alongside several benefits, not least of which is the fact that such companies can return contributed capital to their members much more easily. Furthermore, unlimited companies do not have to make the same number or type of disclosures of financial information as is required of limited companies under the Companies Act 1986.[8]

Private Company

A private company must have a share capital and can be limited or unlimited. The Companies Act 1963 provides for the registration of a private company, typically an undertaking comprising just one member[9] or a family membership. The main advantage of registering as a private company is that it

---

[8] Ss.10 and 11 of the Companies (Amendment) Act 1986.

[9] European Communities (Single Member Private Companies) Regulations 1994 (S.I. No. 275 of 1994).

can avail of concessions under the Companies Acts regarding the disclosure of financial information to the CRO, which must be satisfied that all prerequisites have been met before he issues a certificate of incorporation. In certain circumstances, it can be exempted from the need to have its accounts audited.

Ordinary private citizens are not permitted to subscribe for shares in such companies, the membership of which may not exceed 50 persons.

Where these rules are breached, the company does not automatically lose its private status; rather, its entitlement to the normal privileges merely ceases. However, the courts will deem that a private company has behaved in a criminal manner when it allots its securities or offers shares to members of the public.

Public Limited Company (plc)

Public limited companies can be limited or unlimited. The Companies Act 1983 provides for the establishment of public limited companies or plcs to ensure that small companies which were not private, would not have to comply with a range of duties stemming from the second EC Directive on Company Law. One of the main features of this relatively new type of company is that creditors are protected from loss when the plc is under capitalised or is over-trading. Such a company is limited by shares. A plc has an authorised share capital of at least €38,100.[10] A minimum of 25% of the nominal sum must have been paid on its issued share capital along with any share premium.[11]

Guarantee Company

A guarantee company is commonly found in voluntary,

---

[10] S.19 of the Companies (Amendment) Act 1983.
[11] See chap.3 on *Shares and Shareholders* for further information.

cultural and sporting sectors. It does not have share capital. Instead of being shareholders, its members give guarantees for the unpaid debts. The benefit of setting up such a company is that its liability is limited to the amount which the members have undertaken to contribute to the assets of the company in the event of it being wound up. This is in addition to any amount unpaid on the shares held by members.

MEMORANDUM AND ARTICLES OF ASSOCIATION

The Memorandum and Articles of Association comprise the company law equivalent of a trust deed or a constitution. They create a contractual relationship between the company on one hand and its shareholders. Equally, they represent a contract between the shareholders themselves. Where there is a conflict between the two documents, the Memorandum takes precedence.

Memorandum of Association

This is the company's basic law and includes the regulations that must be followed by its members, who are the people who have shares in the company. The Companies Acts of 1963 and 1983 include Schedules or Memorandum blueprints for the different types of company. For instance, a company limited by shares can use the Memorandum of Association set out in Table B of the First Schedule of the 1963 Act.[12] This type of Memorandum includes the precise details of the name of the company, the objects for which it has been established, the nature and extent of the liability of its members, its share capital and the names, addresses and number of shares of all the company's subscribers.

The 1963 Act requires companies to print its Memorandum and have it duly stamped and signed by each subscriber.

---

[12] See Appendix B at p.165 for a copy of Table B as it appears in the 1963 Act.

Once these signatures are witnessed and attested, the document becomes the company's fundamental law and is filed with the Registrar of Companies.

The Minister for Enterprise, Trade and Employment is authorised to order the changing of a company's name if it is judged to be unsuitable or too similar to that of an existing company. Ministerial approval is required if a company wishes to change its name.

The objects' clause sets out the reasons why the company has been established and it must be expressed in coherent terms in the Memorandum of Association. A company may alter its original objects' clause or replace it with a new one but only after a special resolution has been passed by the members.

The company can engage only in activities, which are mentioned in the objects' clause of its founding statute or Memorandum of Association. If a company tries to enter into transactions, which do not appear in the objects' clause, then it is acting *ultra vires*, which literally means *beyond its powers*.

Generally speaking, objects' clauses are drafted in a broad manner and allow a company to engage in a range of different transactions. But if the court decides that a company has exceeded the generously interpreted terms of its objects' clause, then all such transactions and contracts engaged in may be voided.

So for example, if a company was set up with the object of selling fireplaces, it cannot sell fruit and vegetables unless it amends its objects' clause by special resolution. Neither can the objects' clause be amended with retrospective effect. This was the finding of the House of Lords in the famous case of *Ashbury Railway Carriage Co v. Riche*.[13]

But if a person seeks to rely on an *ultra vires* act on the basis that he was not aware at the time of the transaction that the company was acting beyond its powers, then the

---

[13] (1875) L.R. 7 H.L. 653.

Companies Act 1963 states that such an act may be valid. Furthermore, the EC (Companies) Regulations 1973[14] allow a person dealing in good faith with a non-statutory company to rely on an *ultra vires* transaction entered into by the company.

In recent years, a more liberal approach has been adopted in the interpretation of objects clauses. But the Irish courts have taken an intolerant view of clauses, which are perceived to have been drafted in a deliberately ambiguous manner.

The Memorandum must be clear about the amount of authorised share capital and the manner in which it is apportioned into shares. Under the 1983 Act, public limited companies are required to have an authorised capital of at least €38,100, which can be made up of capital in different currencies, but the denominations must be set out in the Memorandum.

The capital clause in the Memorandum can be changed by way of a resolution of the members at a general meeting but court sanction is needed if the level of capital is to be reduced. But some subscribers, the people who agree to buy shares at the formation of the company, along with certain debenture holders (banks and lending institutions who are creditors rather than shareholders) have recourse to the courts to veto particular proposals to change the objects.

Articles of Association

If the Memorandum of Association is the constitution of the company, then the Articles of Association are its statute law. Put briefly, the document containing the Articles sets out the numbered regulations by which the company is managed, and how relations between the company and its members are to be governed. The rules cover such issues as shares trans-actions, the alteration of capital, the convening of meetings, the appointment and powers of directors and other company

---

[14] S.I. No. 163 of 1973.

officers, the payment of dividends, the publication of accounts and related matters.

As in the case of the Memorandum of Association, the First Schedule of the Companies Act 1963 includes a blueprint for the Articles of Association which is called Table A.[15] Where a company does not have its own tailor-made Articles, it will be assumed that a company has adopted Table A. The vast majority of companies use the model clauses of Table A.

In the event of a company drawing up its own Articles, it is not restricted by the requirements which govern the adoption of the Memorandum of Association and it can amend the Articles by way of special resolution at a general meeting of members. The Articles of Association have statutory power and can be examined by shareholders or by anyone dealing with the company commercially. They are stamped in the same way as a deed and are stamped and signed by each subscriber to the Memorandum of Association.

If the Articles are not stamped, the company in question is trading illegally and the defaulting subscribers may be prosecuted. If the breach is grave and is not remedied in early course, those convicted on indictment can be fined as much as €12,700 and/or be imprisoned for up to five years. If convicted summarily, the penalty can be as high as €1,900 and/or 12 months in jail.

Private companies limited by shares do not have to register their Articles of Association. And where they do not register the Articles, the standard form Articles included in Table A of the First Schedule to the Companies Act 1963 will apply.

A company's Articles of Association may be changed by special resolution of its members – particularly if the change envisaged could lawfully have been included in the original Articles.[16] Such a change requires a majority of at least 75%

---

[15] See Appendix A at p.127 for a copy of Table A as it appears in the 1963 Act.

[16] S.15 of the Companies Act 1963.

of the votes cast at a meeting, notice of which must have been 21 days in advance. But when 21 days notice is not given, a special resolution cannot be passed without the support of 90% of the share value.

Where an amendment involves a clash of interests between the proponents of the change and a group of objecting shareholders, an attempt to alter the Articles will only be successful if it can be shown that it is in the best interests of the company. There is an onus on opponents in these circumstances to show that the proponents were motivated by an improper purpose.[17]

DUTIES OF A COMPANY

As independent legal entities, companies have duties. They are dealt with separately in later chapters but briefly, they are to:

- maintain accurate books of accounts;

- prepare annual accounts;

- carry out an audit each year. Some companies are exempt;

- establish an audit committee;[18]

- file a statement of compliance regarding its policies in relation to the Companies Acts, tax law and all other relevant statutes and regulations including those governing health and safety issues;[19]

- keep registers and other important legal documents;

---

[17] *Gold Reefs* case [1900] 1 Ch. 656 at p.671.

[18] This is a proposal, which is contained in s.40 of the Companies (Auditing and Accounting) Bill 2003 as amended at committee stage. At the time of writing, it is not possible to say whether it will survive the remaining stages before its enactment. In its current form, the requirement will apply to large private companies only.

[19] This is also proposed in s.43 of the Companies (Auditing and Accounting) Bill 2003 as amended at committee stage.

- file papers with the CRO; and

- hold general meetings of the company.

Duty to Maintain Accurate Books of Accounts

Every company must keep proper books of account which should accurately record all company transactions, facilitate an accurate assessment of the company's financial position, allow the accounts to be audited and enable compliance of the balance sheet and profit and loss account with the Companies Acts.

There must be a pattern to the keeping of accounts. In other words, the methods used should be consistent and the timing should be the same, year on year. The accounts should be kept in the company's registered offices or at another location deemed suitable by the directors.

The statutory provisions regarding the maintenance of accounts can be found in section 202 of the 1990 Act. Under this provision, the company's books of account must:

(a) include daily entries of all transaction details and amounts paid into and paid out by the company;

(b) record the assets and liabilities of the company;

(c) record all the services provided by the company together with relevant invoices;

(d) record all goods bought and sold, save for those goods sold for cash in the course of a retail trade. Information must be collated on the identities of the purchasers and sellers; and

(e) include a statement of the stock retained by the company at the end of each financial year.

Duty to Prepare Annual Accounts

Each year, companies must prepare accounts or financial

statements, which are based on the proper books of account. The annual accounts must give a "true and fair view." While this is not legally defined, annual accounts will be deemed to give a true and fair view if they are prepared in accordance with the provisions of the Companies Acts and if they satisfy the standards set down by the Accounting Standards Board. The annual accounts must include:

- a profit and loss account;
- a balance sheet of the company's assets and liabilities;
- a cash flow statement;
- notes which give details regarding figures including in the financial statement; and
- a directors' report.

Duty to Carry Out an Annual Audit

Companies, subject to some narrow exceptions,[20] are obliged to have their annual accounts audited or independently examined by a financial expert. Generally, companies will be exempted if they have a turnover of less than €317,435; balance sheets of less than €1.9 million; staff of less than 50 people; are not a parent or subsidiary company; and have fulfilled their obligations regarding the filing of documents with the CRO. Where an audit is carried out, the auditor is obliged to report to the members of the company, giving his opinion on whether the accounts give a true and fair view.

Duty to Maintain Registers

Companies must keep the following documents:

(a) **Register of Members**. This includes the members'

---

[20] See Pt III of the Companies (Amendment) (No.2) Act 1999.

names, addresses, numbers of shares held and the dates on which members joined or left the company.

(b) **Register of Directors and Secretaries**.[21] This document must record the personal details of directors and company secretaries. In the case of directors, the register must give details of other companies of which they are directors. Any member of the public is entitled to inspect this Register.

(c) **Register of Directors' and Secretaries Interests**. This shows details of any shares, which the directors and the company secretary have in all companies.

(d) **Register of Debenture Holders**. This documents contains details of loans given to the company.

(e) **Minutes of General Meetings**.[22]

(f) **Directors' Service Contracts**.

(g) **Instruments Creating Charges over Company Property**.[23] This record includes details of all borrowings against which parts of the company's assets are offered as security.

(h) **Contracts for the Purchase of Own Shares**. Every member of the public is entitled to inspect this document.

(i) **Register of Interests of Persons in its Shares**. This applies only to public limited companies. Persons who have acquired an interest of more than 5% of the shares of a public limited company must inform the company of same. The company must keep a register of such notifications.

---

[21] S.91 of the Company Law Enforcement Act 2001 amended s.95 of the Companies Act 1963.

[22] S.19 of the Company Law Enforcement Act 2001 amended s.145 of the Companies Act 1963.

[23] S.109 of the Companies Act 1963.

Duty to File Certain Documents with the CRO

Companies must comply with obligations to file with the CRO documents such as the annual return, notice of increase in authorised share capital, change of registered address, notification of the creation of a mortgage or charge, declarations regarding directors, etc. After they are filed, they are free to be inspected by members of the public.

If a company fails to file its annual return or other documents within the prescribed period, it can be subject to a late filing and administrative penalties,[24] **criminal prosecution or strike-off.**

At the time of writing, the provisions relating to administrative fines and penalties have yet to be commenced into law but are expected to be approximately €500.

Duty to hold General Meetings

Apart from single-member private limited companies, every company must hold an annual general meeting. In certain situations, companies must hold extraordinary general meetings.

Failure to fulfil any of these duties is – technically – a criminal offence. If the court finds that a company failed to take reasonable steps to ensure that these obligations be carried out, the directors involved may be prosecuted summarily in the District Court and fined up to €1,900 and/or jailed for up to 12 months.

If they are more serious, they can be tried on indictment in a higher court, which can force a guilty party to pay a penalty of €12,700 and/or serve up to five years jail.

Where the court feels that breaches of the obligations contributed to the company's inability to discharge its debts, directors may be found guilty[25] of an offence. On the

---

[24] S.66 of the Company Law Enforcement Act 2001.
[25] S.203 of the Companies Act 1990.

application of a liquidator or creditor, directors or former directors shall be held personally liable.[26]

If the Court takes the view that the breaches amount to fraudulent trading, a fine of up to €63,000 and/or seven years in jail can be imposed.

---

[26] S.204 of the Companies Act 1990.

CHAPTER 2

Meetings

INTRODUCTION

As a company is an artificial or legal person, it transacts its business by passing resolutions at meetings of its members. For this reason, it is of crucial importance to the proper governance or management of the registered company that meetings be convened and conducted correctly.

Subject to some basic rules set out in the Companies Acts, individual companies can adopt different approaches to the holding of meetings. But at the end of the day, it is the company's shareholders who determine what rules are to be followed in relation to the allocation of votes and the designation of powers to directors. A company's regulations can be changed provided that a sufficient number of shareholders lend support.

DIFFERENT TYPES OF MEETINGS

Annual General Meeting (AGM)

An Annual General Meeting (AGM) must ideally be held once a year and no less frequently than once every 15 months. The main purpose of the AGM is to allow the members an opportunity to discuss the audited accounts and the reports filed by the directors and auditors. Also considered are declarations of dividends, the election of new directors, the appointment of auditors and special business such as amendments to the Memorandum or Articles of Association.

Under the new legislation, a member of a company can apply to the Director of Corporate Enforcement for

an order directing the convening of an AGM where one is overdue.[1]

Extraordinary General Meeting (EGM)

Extraordinary general meetings (EGMs) – or all meetings, which are not AGMs – may also be convened when certain issues need to be urgently discussed.

The directors of a company must call an EGM where the company's assets fall to half or less than half of the called-up share capital.[2]

Class meetings are held when defined groups of members within the company come together to discuss matters of common concern.

Convening Meetings

In normal circumstances, the board of directors calls general meetings. When a meeting is convened in a manner, which is contrary to the Articles of Association, the outcome can be nullified only if the breach is judged to be of considerable significance.

NOTICES

Notice periods required for the convening of meetings differ and are usually stipulated in the Articles of Association. But the 1963 Act sets out the following requirements for notice periods:

- AGM – 21 days;

- EGM – seven days for private companies. This can be shortened where there is agreement from the members and

---

[1] S.131(3) of the Companies Act 1963, as amended by s.14 of the Company Law Enforcement Act 2001.

[2] S.40 of the Companies (Amendment) Act 1983.

their auditor; 14 days for public companies;[3] 21 days for the passing of a special resolution unless 90% of the members agree to a shorter notice period;[4]

- EGMs of private companies with Part II of Table A – seven days;

- Where special resolution is to be passed – 21 days;

- General meeting where there is agreement of auditors and members – any period;

- Extended notice resolutions – less than 21 days where there is agreement of sufficient members as hold 90% of the nominal share value;

- Extended notice of 28 days should be given where there is a resolution proposed to remove a director, unless the Articles of Association make alternative provision;

- Extended notice of 28 days should be given where there is a resolution proposed at an AGM to remove an auditor.

Notices of meetings are to be issued to every member save where it is otherwise stipulated in the Articles of Association.

The default Articles of Table A provide that a meeting shall not be deemed to be invalid where notice has not been received by a member who is eligible to attend or where there has been an accidental omission.

While the Companies Acts are silent on the content of the notices, the Table A Articles state that the notices must inform the recipient of the time, place and general nature of the meeting.

Where the board is unable or refuses to call an AGM, any member may apply to the Director of Corporate Enforcement seeking an order directing that a meeting be held. In relation to EGMs, the 1963 Act allows members representing those

---

[3] S.133 of the Companies Act 1963.
[4] S.141 of the Companies Act 1963.

with at least 10% of the paid up capital and who have voting rights, to ask the board to call such a meeting. If their request is turned down, a meeting may be convened by half those seeking the meeting and ultimately at the expense of those directors who refuse to call the meeting. In relation to the location of meetings, the 1963 Act sets out the following requirements:

- AGM – must be held within the State, unless otherwise provided for in the Articles of Association or where all members agree otherwise; and

- EGM – no restriction on location.

If a company does not hold meetings in accordance with the time and procedural requirements set out in the Acts, the Director of Corporate Enforcement will attempt to persuade it to comply with its obligations as soon as is practicable. If the company rejects this approach, the Director of Corporate Enforcement can initiate criminal prosecution of the directors believed to be responsible for the breaches.

Depending on the seriousness of the breaches, those found guilty on indictment can be fined as much as €12,700 and/or be imprisoned for up to five years. If the default is less serious, summary prosecutions are taken in the District Court which can impose a penalty as high as €1,900 and/or up to 12 months in jail.

RESOLUTIONS

Resolutions are the principal manner by which the company carries on its business at meetings. Notice of resolutions must be circulated to members in sufficient time and they must be clear and precise as to the nature of what is being proposed. There are three types of resolution:

1. **Ordinary resolution.** While there is no formal definition in the Acts or in Table A, an ordinary resolution is taken

to be one requiring a simple majority of the votes cast at a meeting.

2. **Special resolution.** This is defined as one needing a majority of at least 75% of the votes cast at a meeting, notice of which was given at least 21 days in advance.[5] But when notice of less than 21 days is given, a special resolution can be passed when holders of 90% of the value of the voting shares are in agreement.

3. **Extended Notice Resolution.** This resolution is required for important decisions such as the removal of a director or the replacement of auditors. The proposer must give at least 28 days notice to the company. Once the company receives a proposal from a member of the company, it must notify the other members in the same way as it gives notice of meetings. Where it is impracticable to give notice of 21 days, it must advertise in a newspaper circulating in the area in which the company's registered office is situated or use some other method specified in the Articles of Association.

CONDUCT OF MEETINGS

Quorum

Unless otherwise stated in the Articles of Association, the quorum for a private company – providing it is not a one-person company – is two persons. In the case of public companies, at least three people must be present.

In private companies with Table A, meetings must begin with the number of persons required to form a quorum but may continue as long as just one member is present. Meetings must be adjourned for a week or until such time as the directors see fit, if the quorum is not present within a half hour of it starting. Where the members called the meeting, it may be dissolved if the quorum is not filled within this period.

---

[5] S.141 of the Companies Act 1963.

There is statutory provision for a member or director to apply to the High Court for permission to hold a meeting where it is "impracticable" for the quorum to be filled. For instance, where a company has only two members, one of whom holds 51%, the courts have deemed that a meeting may to conducted to allow this member remove the other from the board.

Place

Technological advances have meant that meetings do not have to be held in a given room, office or hall. Meetings may be properly conducted by using audio-visual equipment in overflow rooms.

Role of the Chairman

A meeting of the company should be conducted by the chairman who, under Table A of the Articles of Association, is also the chairman of the board of directors. There is also provision for directors to choose another member of the board. Under Table A, the chairman's powers and duties include:

- The proper conduct of the meeting;
- the power to adjourn the meeting where unruly behaviour prevents him from conducting the meeting in an orderly fashion;
- the power to adjourn the meeting but only with the consent of the members;
- the adjournment of the meeting when he is so directed by the members;
- the casting vote where there is a tie of votes;
- making sure that members are given a fair opportunity to express their views on proposed resolutions;
- the ability to stop discussions on various points once a

reasonable opportunity has been given to express conflicting views;

- ensuring that no wholly new business is transacted at adjourned meetings;

- the ability to allow an amendment to be moved to a proposed resolution as long as the amendment is within the scope of the notice given; and

- the fair and proper conduct of voting.

Voting

Only registered members of the company can vote. According to the standard Articles, resolutions may be passed by a simple show of hands. Subject to certain exceptions in relation to the rights of minorities and other specified classes of members, members may exercise their franchise for whatever reasons they wish. They are even allowed to ignore the perceived greater interests of the company.

The chairman can choose a poll or a show of hands as a way of determining the meeting's views on any proposed resolution. Often, a poll will be called when a show of hands throws up an inconclusive result or a narrow victory for one side.

The chairman is obliged to carry out a poll if any member, with the support of two other members present or with the support of at least 10% of total voting rights, so requests. In relation to the vote, the chairman can decide:

- At what stage during the meeting it will take place;

- how it will take place; and

- which members of the company can vote.

The right of a member to call for a ballot can be qualified by the express terms in the Articles of Association only in relation to the election of a chairman and resolutions which relate to adjournments.

Proxy Votes

Any member who is allowed to attend and vote at a meeting of the company may appoint another person as their proxy to speak and vote for them in a ballot or in a show of hands. A member of a company may appoint more than one proxy, unless the Articles of Association specifically disallow it. According to the rules regarding proxies set out in the Articles of Association in Table A:

- the instrument of appointment of a proxy must be signed by the shareholder or his authorised agent;

- the instrument of appointment of a proxy must be stamped with a company seal where the shareholder is a company;

- the instrument must be delivered to the company's registered office or such other specified place at least 48 hours before the meeting;

- a person who is both a member and a proxy can vote only once on a show of hands;

- a properly appointed proxy is allowed to requisition a poll;

- a properly appointed proxy is entitled to speak on behalf of the represented member;

- the votes of properly appointed proxies shall be deemed valid unless the proxy is insane, their authority as proxies is revoked or the shareholder dies;

- a proxy is not bound to vote unless there is a stipulation to the contrary; and

- all directors who are appointed proxies must cast their votes.

The company will pay the expenses incurred in sending out information designed to persuade shareholders or their proxies to vote in a certain way. Unlike in the case of the State, the company does not have to include in this information, the view of those shareholders who are against their proposed resolutions. But the costs may not be paid where the information is misleading or where the resolution being proposed by the company is one which favours the interests of the directors.

Minutes

The proceedings of all general meetings must be recorded in a minute book and signed by the person who chaired the meeting. The minutes are regarded as an accurate account of what transpired at the meeting in question. The minutes are open to inspection by any member and may be copied.

If a company is found to have disregarded its obligations in relation to the conduct of meetings, guilty directors can be prosecuted summarily.

If convicted, the penalty can be as high as €1,900 and/or 12 months in jail. If the default is more serious, the prosecution can be taken on indictment and the guilty directors can be fined as much as €12,700 and/or be imprisoned for up to five years.

CHAPTER 3

Shares and Shareholders

The members of the company are the people who are the original subscribers to the company's Memorandum of Association. Inasmuch, they comprise the group, which participates in the capital of the company. Anyone who subsequently buys shares also becomes a member of the company. The list of members is kept on a register, which includes all of their personal details including information relating to the number of shares they hold.

Shares have been defined by a leading legal author and commercial lawyer, Thomas Courtney, as an intangible accumulation of rights, interests and obligations. Shares comprise the interest of a shareholder in the company and that interest is measured by a sum of money. A member of a company limited by shares is a shareholder.

FEATURES OF SHARES

- Shares confer rights and obligations under contract.
- Shares are transferable by using methods, which are provided in the Articles of Association.
- Shares can be protected, not in a physical manner but through legal means.
- Shares are held by members of a company and so, they constitute an interest in the company itself, rather than an interest in the company's assets.
- Shares confer statutory duties and privileges and also constitutional duties. For instance, shares determine a shareholder's right to vote at company meetings and they confer a right to be paid sums of money from liquidated assets.

- Each share has a nominal or par value calculated by dividing the total share capital by the number of shares. For instance, if the share capital of a company is €500,000 and there are 100,000 shares, the par value will be €5. It is a measure of the shareholder's interest in the company and it also a measure of the shareholder's liability to the company. The nominal value does not always equate to the real value of the shares.

- A share certificate is issued to shareholders within two months of allotment or lodgment of a transfer. The share certificate bears a seal and information about the amount of shares and the money paid.

- The share certificate is a declaration by the company that the bearer owns a specific number of shares. It is neither a deed nor a negotiable document. The company is indemnified for loss which results from forgery.

- All shares within a particular class are ranked equally. This is known as *pari passu.*

- The subscribers to the company agree to become members and they agree to buy shares. Before receiving their shares, the names of all the subscribers to the Memorandum must be entered on the register of members.

Failure to enter the names on the register constitutes a criminal act. Defaulting directors will in the first instance be notified of the Director of Corporate Enforcement's concern.

If the breach continues, summary prosecutions can be taken in the District Court and a penalty as high as €1,900 and/or 12 months in jail can be handed down. More serious transgressions can prompt prosecutions on indictment, which can involve fines of up to €12,700 and/or jail terms of up to five years.

If the Court forms the view that the breaches are so grave as to constitute fraudulent trading, a fine of €63,000 and/or a jail sentence of up to seven years may be imposed.

SHARE ALLOTMENT

Directors give authority for the issue of shares but not without the permission of a general meeting of the company or unless there is provision within the Articles of Association.[1] When conferring authority on directors to allot shares, the shareholders must cite a maximum number of shares to be issued and a date before which they are to be issued. The maximum time period is five years from the date of the resolution to allot shares.

Directors must allot their shares *bona fide* and in the best interests of the company. The courts have struck down allotments which were made by directors in order to secure their own positions. The situation in relation to resisting takeover bids is less clear. Consideration is given to whether the directors were acting in the best interests of the company.

The allotment of shares is subject to normal rules of contract law. The company is obliged to inform the Registrar of Companies within one month of the allotment, giving details of the shareholders' names, addresses, number of shares bought and amounts paid and owing.

Existing ordinary shareholders have the right of first refusal on the issue of new shares within a period of 21 days from the offer.[2] Statutory pre-emption rights are not allowed to holders of preference shares or to members of employee share option schemes. These rights are not afforded when the shares are to be paid for either wholly or partly in non-cash terms. Regardless, pre-emption rights may be nullified by provisions in the Memorandum of Association or by the Articles of Association.

Breaches of section 23 render the company and every officer who was aware of the contravention, jointly and severally liable to the person who should have received an offer.

Persons found guilty of being in breach of their obligations

---

[1] S.20 of the Companies (Amendment) Act 1983.

[2] S.23 of the Companies (Amendment) Act 1983.

under this provision can on indictment, be fined as much as €12,700 and/or be imprisoned for up to five years. If convicted summarily, the penalty can be as high as €1,900 and/or 12 months in jail.

Shares may be issued at a premium but not at a discount. Because the nominal value of the issued shares only rarely reflects the real value of the company, it is normal for small companies to issue shares at a premium. The proceeds of the issue of premium shares are lodged in a separate share premium account and are regarded, not as profit but as capital. The premium is the difference in the value of the shares given in consideration for allotted shares and the nominal value.

Shares can be allotted for cash or for some other form of consideration, all of which does not need to be paid on allotment. Shareholders who have unpaid shares may be liable if the company calls in the balance. If the company agrees, shares may be paid in non-cash terms such as expertise or goodwill. The Companies Registration Office (CRO) needs to be informed when shares are paid for in non-cash terms. There are restrictions on the type of non-cash consideration, which a plc may accept. Furthermore, that consideration must be independently valued.

CLASSES OF SHARES

The Memorandum of Association or the Articles of Association must provide for the creation of different types of shares. Table A companies can create different shares with different privileges and obligations but there must be equality between shareholders within the same class.

Ordinary Shares

These are the most common type of shares and – depending on how the company performs – they carry the potential for the greatest return and the greatest risk.

Bonus Shares

These shares are issued in what is little more than an accountancy procedure. They are issued when a company capitalises its profits, revenue reserves or some other funds in order to pay out bonus shares. They are given to existing members in accordance with their entitlement to dividends.

Preference Shares

These shares carry preferential rights in relation to the dividend, capital and voting. Typically, they carry no voting rights or no rights to participate in any surplus on the winding up of the company.

In relation to the dividend, the holder of preferential shares is normally paid his dividend before any ordinary shareholder. The dividend is expressed as a percentage of the nominal value of the share each year. Unless the terms of the issue state the contrary, the dividend is payable only when a dividend is declared. Again, unless it is stated to the contrary, preferential rights regarding the dividend are cumulative if a dividend is not declared or if there is a shortfall in the payment of a dividend declared in a previous year. Arrears due to preferential shareholders take priority over dividends owing to ordinary shareholders.

When the preference aspect of the share relates to capital, the preferential shareholder has, on the winding up of the company, his capital investment repaid before ordinary shareholders receive their investment. Preferential voting rights can be given to some shareholders in this class.

Deferred Shares

Also known as founders' shares, they relate to special rights given to the initial members of the company. They scarcely exist in modern companies.

Redeemable Shares

Redeemable shares are almost like loans to the company.

Employee Shares

The Finance Act of 1982 introduced employee shares. They have become increasingly popular in recent years as ways of encouraging greater efficiency from and the co-operation of staff prior to the flotation of semi-state companies. Shares can be:

- Allotted directly by the company to the member who is then registered;

- transferred from an existing member to a new member who is then registered;

- involuntarily transferred to a new member from a member who dies or is declared bankrupt; and

- transferred to a person by estoppel, i.e. when his name is wrongly put on the register and he is deemed to have assented by his delay in rectifying the error

WHO CAN OWN SHARES?

- Natural persons.

- Minors: they can inherit or buy shares with full rights but they can repudiate their membership any time before their 18th birthday.

- Companies, provided the Memorandum of Association and the Articles of Association so allow. But there are restrictions on a company owning its own shares or shares in its holding company.

- Foreigners.

- Bankrupts.

- Persons of unsound mind.

SHARE CONVERSION

By way of ordinary resolution and with the normal notification and disclosure obligations being fulfilled, Table A companies can convert blocks of shares into stock if shares are fully paid up. Shares can also be consolidated. It is uncommon today but consolidation can happen when old companies have a large number of shares of little value. The shares are converted into one larger share of aggregate value. It is possible to convert shares into redeemable shares as long as the required changes are made to the Memorandum of Association and the Articles of Association.[3] The nominal value of non-redeemable issued share capital must be at least 10% of the total issued share capital. It is illegal to convert a member's shareholding without his permission.

Table A companies can place a *lien*, or right to withhold possession, on shares which have not been paid up. After 14 days notice to the shareholder, the company can sell the shares.

When a shareholder fails to pay up on shares he holds, the directors of Table A companies have the power to cancel or forfeit the shares. Equally, there is nothing to stop a shareholder simply surrendering his shares to the company.

SHARE TRANSFER

A share is regarded in the Companies Acts as personal goods, ownership of which may be transferred in accordance with the guidelines contained in the Articles of Association – unlike real estate.[4] This means that a deed of transfer is not required and the ownership of shares can change without any implications for the legal status of the company.

A proper instrument of transfer must be delivered to the transferee, who is the person acquiring the shares. The

---

[3] S.207 of the Companies Act 1990.
[4] S.79 of Companies Act 1963.

instrument states the name of the transferor, who is the person allotting the shares, as well as the name of the transferee and the number of shares. Share certificates are then delivered to the transferee. The transaction must be noted in the Register of Members. Share transfers are subject to 1% stamp duty.

Subject to pre-emption rules and the company's Articles of Association, shares in a private company are freely transferable. The restrictions contained in the Articles reflect the fact that many Irish companies are small and often run by families. The transferee has equitable rights as a shareholder before the transfer is registered. But the onus is on him – and not on the transferor – to execute the transfer as quickly as possible. Prior to registration, the transferee has no right to vote at meetings but may be able to direct the transferor to vote according to his wishes. The correct procedure is as follows:

1. After signing the share certificate and the transfer form, the transferor sends the two documents to the company.

2. The company keeps the share certificate and returns the stamped transfer form to the transferor.

3. The transferee pays the transferor who returns the stamped transfer form to the transferee.

4. After stamping the transfer form, the transferee returns it to the company.

5. The company registers the transferee on the Register of Members and sends a share certificate to the transferee.

6. The company makes an amendment to the transferor's share certificate and its share records.

7. The company sends the amended share certificate to the transferor.

REFUSAL TO REGISTER A TRANSFER

The directors have the right to refuse registration if so allowed by the Articles of Association. They may refuse registration if the transfer was not in compliance with the Articles. Directors can refuse to register a share transfer without giving an explanation.[5] But they must show they are acting *bona fide* and in the best interests of the company. Forged transfers are null and void and the company can claim compensation from persons who use forged documents in the transfer of shares. Case law has shown that directors need to meet a high standard of proof in order to convince the court that their decisions to refuse registration are in the best interests of the company.

The power to refuse registration must be exercised quickly. A period of two months is regarded as reasonable because this is the statutory period within which the transferee must be informed.

As legal ownership of the shares does not pass until the transfer is registered, the transferor remains as a trustee for the transferee and is not liable for any claim during that period. He must pay an accumulated dividend, vote in accordance with the instructions of the equitable owner and must assist in the execution of the transfer and the handing over of the share certificate.

Transmission on Death or Bankruptcy

When a shareholder dies, shares automatically vest in his personal representative. Either a Grant of Probate or Letters of Administration are sufficient proof of the shareholder's death. The personal representative, while not becoming a member, may be registered as a member or may transfer the shares. In relation to jointly held shares, the surviving owner becomes the sole owner.

When a shareholder is declared bankrupt, the trustee may be registered as a member and may transfer or disclaim shares,

---

[5] Art.3 of Table A of the Articles of Association.

depending on whether the shares are worth having. Beneficial ownership passes to the trustee although the shareholder does not cease to be a member of the company. Altering the Articles of Association may change this.

Shareholders' Rights

A shareholding comprises a bundle of rights, which are exercisable in proportion to the size of the entire shareholding. A shareholder has a right to:

- be maintained in membership – as long as his details are registered;

- receive payment of a dividend once a dividend has been declared. There are further restrictions in the case of public limited companies;[6]

- vote at meetings. This vote is qualified depending on the class of share;

- participate in any surplus assets after the company is liquidated and when all the creditors are paid off – as long as the shares confer this right;

- receive notice of general meetings unless precluded by the Articles of Association;

- receive a copy of the accounts;

- receive a copy of the Memorandum of Association and the Articles of Association;

- receive minutes of general meetings;

- inspect the register of members;

- participate in the winding up of the company. Once creditors and the liquidator has been paid off, the shareholder has a

---

[6] Dividends can only be paid out here, where the net assets, after the distribution, are more than the aggregate of its called-up share capital and its undistributable reserves.

call on the remaining funds which is proportionate to the shareholding;

- apply to have an inspector appointed to the company;[7]

- serve notice on the company or any of its officers of a default in compliance with the provisions of the Companies Acts. Unless the problem is resolved within 14 days, the member can apply to the High Court for an order directing that the company or its officers make good the default.[8] The Director of Corporate Enforcement also has the power to make such an application;

- apply to the CRO to have its company restored. Under the new legislation,[9] a company can be struck off for failing to make an annual return, failing to make a statement of its particulars to the Revenue Commissioners or where the company is not carrying on business. In this situation, the directors, officers and members are as liable as they would be, had the company not been struck off. But on the application of a shareholder,[10] the CRO can restore the company if it is satisfied that all outstanding documents have been filed and all liabilities settled; and

- petition for relief where shareholders are being oppressed.[11] The High Court shall grant such relief where it believes that the affairs of the company are being conducted in a

---

[7] S.7 of the Companies Act 1990, as amended by s.20 of the Company Law Enforcement Act 2001. Qualifying members include either 100 members of a company or members holding at least 10% of the paid up share capital. In the case of a company without a share capital, the requirement is for at least 20% of members.

[8] S.371 of the Companies Act 1963, as amended by s. 96 of the Company Law Enforcement Act 2001.

[9] S.12B(1) of the Companies (Amendment) Act 1982 as inserted by s.46 of the Company Law Enforcement Act 2001.

[10] S.12C(1)of the Companies (Amendment) Act 1982 as inserted by s. 46 of the Company Law Enforcement Act 2001.

[11] S.205 of the Companies Act 1963.

manner, which is considered burdensome, harsh and wrong. The court will distinguish such a petition from an application from shareholders comprising a minority, to simply overturn a decision, which has been ratified by a majority of members.

While shareholders have the rights enumerated above, it is a fundamental rule of Company Law that the majority rules – subject to the section 205 caveat regarding the oppression of minority shareholders. When the majority rules, the minority are often dissatisfied. Generally, the courts maintain an anti-interventionist approach. Notwithstanding their reluctance to intervene in the internal decisions of companies, the courts are anxious to ensure that the majority acts *bona fide*.

The basic rule in relation to remedies is that when a wrong has allegedly been committed in the course of the company's business, the company should bring proceedings and not the aggrieved shareholder. No individual can sue when the transaction involved is supported by a simple majority of the members because it is the policy of the company.

These two principles were enunciated in a landmark case, which has given its name to the Rule in *Foss v. Harbottle*.[12] A shareholder who has difficulty with a decision of the company must route his complaint through the company itself. Underlining this rule is the principle that the company is separate from its shareholders. The directors have been delegated by the shareholders to manage the company. To this rule, there are currently six exceptions:

1. when the act complained of by the shareholder is *ultra vires* or illegal;

2. where the aggrieved shareholder's "personal and individual" rights have been invaded;

---

[12] (1843) 2 Hare 461.

3.   where the need for a "special majority" or procedure has been disregarded;

4.   where the majority of the company have perpetrated a fraud on the minority;

5.   where there is oppression of a minority;[13] or

6.   where a shareholder brings a petition for the winding up of the company on "just and equitable" grounds.[14]

In each of the situations above, the shareholder can be the plaintiff rather than the company. But these exceptions must be distinguished from cases were the Rule in *Foss v Harbottle* has no application.

In relation to section 205 cases, any member who complains that the affairs of the company are being conducted or that the powers of the company are being exercised in a manner oppressive to or in disregard of him or any of the other members, he may apply to the court for an order preventing such behaviour.

The substantive criteria for grounding such actions are broad. Members or the personal representatives, frequently their next of kin, may bring proceedings, which can be heard *in camera* in order to avoid serious prejudice to the legitimate interests of the company. Furthermore, the courts have a wide range of remedies from which to choose. Oppressive behaviour includes acts, which are burdensome, harsh and wrongful. One act of oppression is sufficient grounds. The Irish courts have been less inclined to strike out section 205 actions than have the English courts with similar actions.

---

[13] S.205 of the Companies Act 1963.

[14] S.213(f) of the Companies Act 1963.

INSIDER DEALING

Insider Dealing is dealt with in another chapter.[15] But briefly, insider dealing or unlawful dealing is a criminal offence and defined as the dealing in the company's shares, debentures or other debt securities by persons who are connected with the company and are in possession of confidential sensitive information.[16] Insiders include persons who within the preceding six months, have been directors, shadow directors, company secretaries, employees, auditors, liquidators, receivers, examiners, persons administering a compromise or scheme with creditors, shareholders, officers of substantial shareholders and persons who because of a professional, business or other relationship with the company, would reasonably be expected to have access to sensitive confidential information.

If the Court concludes that someone in one of the categories above has engaged in insider dealing, the affected parties can prosecute compensation claims.

The Director of Corporate Enforcement can initiate a prosecution, which can lead to the imposition on guilty directors and company officers of heavy penalties. On summary conviction, the fines can be up to €1,900 and/or 12 months in jail.[17] But because this crime is regarded so seriously, prosecutions on indictment are more likely. The fine can be as high as €254,000 and/or ten years imprisonment.

---

[15] See Chap.4 on *Directors' Duties*.

[16] S.108 of the Companies Act 1990.

[17] S.114 of the Companies Act 1990 as amended by s.104 of the Company Law Enforcement Act 2001.

CHAPTER 4

Creditors

The creditors of a company are the group of persons and institutions to whom money is owed by the company. In many ways, they are a vulnerable group because they are exposed to the difficulties encountered by companies to which they have lent money for investment or other purposes. But there are ways in which creditors can limit their exposure in situations where companies experience trading difficulties. Creditors fall into two categories:

1. **Secured Creditors** This group comprises persons whose debts are secured to one or more of the company's assets. For example, if an investor lends a large sum of money to a small manufacturer, he may require the deeds of the company's property as security for his loan. He may also secure the right to have a receiver appointed in circumstances where he has to force the repayment of his loan.[1]

2. **Unsecured Creditors** Unsecured creditors lend money without any attachment being made to the company's assets. If the company finds itself in serious financial difficulty, the unsecured creditors must await repayment until after the debts to the secured creditors have been discharged.

Creditors' Powers

A creditor has the power to have the company liquidated so that he can have his debt repaid.

---

[1] See Chap.8 on *Receivers*.

- He can do this by **applying to the High Court.**[2] In order to successfully petition for a liquidator to be appointed, the creditor must show that a debt of at least €1,270 has been unpaid for three weeks or more, despite written requests for the debt to be repaid. Alternatively, the creditor must show that a court judgment has not been satisfied or where the court receives other strong evidence, which supports the claim that the company cannot pay its debts.[3]

- Alternatively, a **Creditors' Voluntary Liquidation** may take place.[4] This happens when the members of the company pass a resolution at a general meeting to wind up the company voluntarily because it cannot pay its debts. On the same day that they pass this resolution, they call a meeting of the creditors. This meeting must be advertised and notice of ten days must be given to affected creditors. At the meeting, the directors must circulate a full list of the creditors and give details of the debts owed to each. The statement of affairs, which is prepared by the directors, is debated and a Committee of Inspection may be appointed. This committee supervises the work of the liquidator, should one be nominated by the meeting of the members. If a majority of the creditors by value prefer to nominate their own liquidator, then their wish prevails over that of the members of the meeting.

A creditor has the power to have a receiver appointed when a company has failed to pay its secured creditors. This can be done on foot of the terms of the debenture or by making an application to the High Court.[5]

---

[2] S.213 of the Companies Act 1963 as amended by para.17, Sch.1 of the Companies (Amendment) Act 1983 and s.93 of the Company Law Enforcement Act 2001.

[3] S.214 of the Companies Act 1963 as amended by s.123 of the Companies Act 1990.

[4] S.266 Companies Act 1963 as amended by s.130 of the Companies Act 1990.

[5] See Chap.8 on *Receivers*.

A creditor has the power to have an examiner appointed.[6] When an examiner is appointed, an effort is made to rescue the company from its difficulties. In this process, a creditor can apply to the High Court when he feels that the company is unlikely or unable to pay its debts, where there is no liquidation or when the court is persuaded that there is a good chance that the company can recover from its financial difficulties.

A creditor can call on the company to make good its default on the repayment of its debts. If the company fails to remedy the default within 14 days, the creditor can apply to the High Court for an order directing that the debt be repaid.[7]

A creditor has the power to apply for an order of the court giving judgment in respect of unpaid debts. The court can consider a number of different ways of enforcing this judgment including the engagement of the services of the Sheriff.

If a creditor has problems securing the repayment of money lent, he can also ask the High Court to appoint one or more inspectors to examine the company's business and write a report on same.[8] In these situations, the court may ask the creditor to lodge a sum of money in court as security to cover the costs of the investigation.[9] The court determines the scope and method of the investigation to be carried out by the inspectors.

When a creditor has not succeeded in executing a judgement for a debt owed by a company, which is not in liquidation, he can apply for a range of other reliefs.[10] Included among them are orders for:

- the arrest of a contributory director, shadow director, company officer;

---

[6] See Chap.7 on *Examinership*.

[7] S.371 of the Companies Act 1963.

[8] S.7 of the Companies Act 1990.

[9] The court may look for security of at least €6,350 and not more than €317,000.

[10] S.251 of the Companies Act 1990.

- the seizure of relevant company documents;

- the inspection of the company's books and records;

- the examination on oath of company officers in relation to the company's business;

- directing that contributions be made to the insolvent company by relating companies;

- the return of assets, which were sold in situations where they should not have been disposed of;

- the imposition of personal liability on a director for fraudulent or reckless trading;

- for declaration of failure to keep proper books of account; and

- the assessment of damages for breaches of the Companies Acts.

A creditor can apply to have a company restored to the Register of Companies where it has been struck off because it has failed to make an annual return. This can be done in order to help the creditor recover the money owed to him. Such orders can also be made by the High Court when the company has been struck off because it was not carrying on business or where it deems it to be fair that it be restored. In these situations, the company continues in existence as if nothing happened.

CHAPTER 5

Directors: Appointment, Removal and Remuneration

INTRODUCTION

The shareholders of a company select directors to manage the company. They can be removed by a simple majority of the shareholders. Directors have a wide range of obligations to their shareholders. These obligations are known as fiduciary duties because they relate to the requirements of the director as an agent or trustee for the interests of shareholders. Given the directors' special position within the company, the Companies Acts contain complex rules, which govern transactions between directors. The Acts include provisions for the disclosure of those transactions.

Typically, a small firm has a board of directors consisting of a managing director, salaried executive directors, paid non-executive directors and a company secretary. In larger companies, specific management functions are often given to sub-committees and in some cases, companies sign management contracts with external consultants who run their business. The extent to which directors can delegate their powers is governed by the Articles of Association.

Generally speaking, companies are free to draw up their own regulations regarding the manner of the appointment, operation and removal of directors – subject of course to requirements set out in the Companies Acts, among which stipulate that all companies must have at least two directors[1] and a company secretary.[2]

---

[1] S.174 of the Companies Act 1963.
[2] S.175 of the Companies Act 1963.

If they don't, those company members suspected of being in contravention of the Companies Acts will be asked by the Director of Corporate Enforcement to address the problem. If he is ignored, the Director of Corporate Enforcement can bring a prosecution in the District Court, which can impose a maximum penalty of €1,900 and/or a jail term of not more than 12 months. The toughest penalty, if convicted on indictment, may be a fine of €12,700 and/or a prison sentence of five years.

These maximum penalties – imposed following summary conviction and conviction on indictment – apply to all situations discussed below where there breaches of the legal requirements are found to have taken place.

In the Table A of the Articles of Association, the directors are given the general power to manage the business of the company. Indeed, the managing director may have specific powers delegated to him.

But a company can opt for its own Articles, which can also impose heavy obligations on directors. For instance, it is possible for the Articles to require directors to seek support from their members in order to get approval for borrowing.

If a company is found to be in breach of its own Articles of Association, the Director of Corporate Enforcement encourages it to comply with its own rules. If the breach is such as to constitute fraudulent trading or an attempt to defraud creditors, then he can initiate a legal process, which may end in criminal prosecutions on indictment.[3]

TYPES OF DIRECTORS

The Managing Director

The managing director is the person who conducts most of the daily business on behalf of the company. If the company is using Table A, the managing director:

---

[3] S.297 of the Companies Act 1963.

- is a member of the company, who is appointed by the board;

- has his terms of service set by the board;

- does not have to retire in accordance with a rota system;

- may be given such powers as the board decides, including all powers to run the company on a provisional basis; and

- is not automatically allowed to represent the company in court.

The Company Secretary

While there are no established qualifications for holding the office of company secretary, every company must have one. His principal function is to make sure that the company's affairs are conducted in accordance with the Companies Acts and with its own Articles of Association.

In a private company, there are no qualifications required for a Company Secretary. But in a public limited company, the directors must make sure that the Company Secretary has the knowledge and experience required to carry out the functions.[4] In this regard, the basic requirements for a company secretary are that he:

- have the "requisite knowledge and experience" to discharge his functions;

- have been a company secretary during three of the five years before his appointment or be a member of the Chartered Institute of Secretaries or any of the other bodies recognised by the Minister for Enterprise, Trade and Employment;

- not have a conviction for an offence involving fraud or undischarged bankrupts;

- not have been a director of an insolvent company; and

---

[4] S.236 of the Companies Act 1990.

- is appointed by designation in the statement given to the Registrar of Companies together with the Memorandum of Association.

If he is in breach of any of these conditions, both he and the company are liable to be prosecuted by the Director of Corporate Enforcement summarily or on indictment.

Under Table A, the secretary may:

- be appointed and removed by the directors and on terms and conditions set by the directors;

- in the case of the first Company Secretary of a company, he must be named in papers filed with the Companies Registration Office when the company is incorporated;

- have his terms and conditions determined by the directors;

- be one of the directors but must avoid acting in a dual capacity;

- have a beneficial shareholding but must keep same available for inspection at the company's registered office; and

- participate in more general decisions regarding the management of the company.

The Company Secretary's principal duty is to ensure that the company complies with the Companies Acts. In this regard, they must:

- sign the annual accounts which are sent to the registrar of companies;

- issue debenture certificates;

- deliver to the CRO a return of allotments;

- keep minutes of general meetings and records of shareholders, debenture-holders charges, directors and secretaries;

- send out copies of the balance sheet as well as the reports from auditors and directors;

- verify the statement of a company's affairs if court liquidation is likely;

- verify the statement of a company's affairs given to a receiver appointed by debenture holders with floating charges; and

- ensure that the company's requirements in relation to VAT are fulfilled.

In addition, they have obligations, which extend over four areas.

Statutory duties

These comprise obligations, which are shared between the Company Secretary and the directors. They include the duty:

- to sign the annual return;

- to certify that the financial statements accompanying the annual return are true copies of the originals;

- to draw up a statement of affairs in companies, which are being wound up or are in receivership, to sign applications forms, which accompany the statutory declaration for companies which are re-registering; and

- to make a statutory declaration needed before a public limited company can carry on business.

Disclosure duties

The Company Secretary must disclose all relevant information for inclusion in the Register of Directors and Secretaries and the Register of Directors' and Secretary's Interests. This information covers such areas as the name, address and details of any share interests.

Duty to exercise due care, skill and diligence

The Company Secretary can be held responsible for any loss arising from his negligence. The skill level required will depend on his level of knowledge or experience.

Administrative duties

Depending on the size of the company, the Company Secretary must fulfil a range of administrative duties, which include:

- taking and maintaining minutes of meetings of the board, board sub-committees and general meetings;

- keeping custody of the company seal, which is used to endorse all important company documents;

- maintaining for inspection a company register which includes a list of all members, directors, secretaries and their interests;

- making sure that documents are submitted to the CRO within the set time limits;

- notifying members of meetings and their agendas;

- ensuring that members receive copies of all resolutions;

- ensuring that the company's name is fixed legibly and in a conspicuous place and that the company's letterhead includes all the requisite details;

- publishing statutory notices;

- administering share transfers;

- making sure that directors have adequate legal and administrative back-up;

- communicating decisions of the board to members; and

- depending on the type of company, swearing affidavits, interviewing job applicants, signing cheques and other such administrative functions.

Where a Company Secretary is found to have knowingly made a statement or signed a document which contains incorrect or misleading information, or where he has been reckless in the conduct of his duties, he will be in breach of the Companies Acts and can be prosecuted by the Director of Corporate Enforcement summarily or on indictment.

Shadow Directors

A shadow director is a person whose instructions are implemented by the other directors of the company.[5] Since the enactment of the 1990 Act, they have been regarded as the same as company directors. While not a member of the board of directors, a shadow director is significantly involved in the running of the company. From a distance, he dictates to someone who is an actual director, how he wants the company to be managed. Before 1990, the shadow director did not bear the same liabilities and obligations as did the other directors. Now they carry the same onerous duties across a range of areas including fraudulent or reckless trading.[6] As a result of this Act, a shadow director came under an obligation to disclose in writing to the company, any interest he has in contracts or proposed contracts with the company.[7]

---

[5] S.27 of the Companies Act 1990. Excepted from this definition are persons who tender professional advice and directions to company directions.

[6] S.150 of the Companies Act 1990 made shadow directors liable to restriction in the event that they fail to act in accordance with the highest standards. S.138 of the 1990 Act amended s.297 of the principal Act in that it imposes liability on a shadow director who is deemed to have behaved in a reckless or fraudulent manner in his role as an officer of the company.

[7] S.27(3) of the Companies Act 1990. This brought shadow directors under s.194 of the Companies Act 1963, which sets out the duties of directors in relation to the disclosure of interests in contracts or proposed contracts with the company.

If a shadow director fails to disclose an involvement he may have in business he is carrying out with the company of which he is a shadow director, then he is liable to prosecution by the Director of Corporate Enforcement.

Alternate Directors

The Articles of Association in Table A permit that a person may be appointed as an alternate director on a stand-in basis. He can be appointed only with the agreement of a majority of the directors and also by a special resolution. Once appointed, the alternate director is entitled to get notices of meetings and to cast votes.

De Facto Directors

Persons are sometimes regarded as directors of a company when they have not been properly appointed. Ultimately, much depends on the circumstances of the company and the degree to which the *de facto* director is actually involved, but it is important to note that directors in this category may be the subject of restrictment applications under section 150 of the Companies Act 1990.

Directors' Families

A director must disclose to the company if his wife or any of his children have acquired a beneficial interest in the company's shares. When a director is disqualified from taking positions such as liquidator or auditor, "connected persons" in other words his spouse, parent, brother, sister and children, are also disqualified. This is a special feature of the 1990 Act.[8]

---

[8] S.63 of the Companies Act 1990.

APPOINTMENT OF DIRECTORS

The Companies Acts set out the manner in which only the first directors are appointed to the board of a company. The subscribers to the Memorandum of Association identify at least two people as directors before registering a company. The directors in question must give detailed statements about their own affairs to the Registrar of Companies and must in writing consent to act as directors.

Where directors fail to do this, the validity of their appointments may be challenged and if the Director of Corporate Enforcement deems fit, he may initiate a summary prosecution or prosecution on indictment.

Where these directors qualify for shares, the entitlement must be taken up within two months. Votes on the appointment of new directors must be taken individually. This is to prevent an abuse of process by some parties who may wish to increase the chances of a controversial or unpopular appointment being made by including it among a bigger number of more acceptable choices voted in en bloc. Directors who work in the company on a full-time executive basis are employees of the company.

Once the first directors are appointed, companies can choose whatever methods they wish when selecting new board members. Thereafter, the company can stipulate particular methods in its Articles of Association for choosing directors or it can ensure that the Articles of Association designate particular persons or shareholders to act as directors or to select directors.

At least one of the directors of a company must be resident within the State.[9] Excepted from this rule are companies, which hold a bond of €25,395, the purpose of which is to provide for payment of any penalties, which might be imposed

---

[9] S.43 of the Companies (Amendment) (No. 2) Act 1999.

for breaches of the Companies Acts. In relation to companies adopting Table A:

- The directors must fix the size of the board by general meeting.

- The directors may increase or reduce the number of directors by general meeting.

- The directors may decide the manner in which directors retire by rotation.

- No qualifying shares are needed but such a qualification may be set down by general meeting. The rationale behind qualifying shares is that directors with a financial stake in the concern are likely to take a keener interest in the running of the company than non-investor directors.

- Notice of between three and 21 days must be given to the shareholders of the intention to appoint a new director.

- Notice of the proposed director's willingness to serve must also be given, save where he is recommended by existing directors or where the proposed director is due to retire by rotation but wants to be re-elected.

- Unless the general meeting resolves not to re-appoint a director who is due to retire by rotation but wants to be re-elected, he shall be deemed to be re-elected.

- Directors can fill casual vacancies with persons who serve until the next AGM at which point, this person will be eligible for re-election.

- Where the full quota of directorships is not filled, the directors or the members can fill any vacancy temporarily.

The courts have stated that where no AGM is held, there is a risk that the directors will be deemed to have retired by rotation but they remain in office until the AGM is held.

Limitation

A person is prohibited from being a director of more than 25 companies.[10] For the purposes of this limitation, exceptions will apply in relation to directorships of companies involved in long-term economic activity within the State and public companies, whether limited or unlimited. Investment companies, banking institutions and certain companies quoted on the Stock Exchange are also exempted.

Restriction and Disqualification

Before the issues of restriction and disqualification are discussed, it is worth noting that the Employment Equality Act 1998 prohibits discrimination against directors on the grounds of sex, marital or family status, age, disability, religion, sexual orientation, race or membership of the travelling community.

Legally, there is nothing to prevent persons becoming directors who are infants, senile, illiterate or innumerate.

Table A companies prohibit bankrupts and persons of unsound mind from serving as directors.[11] In relation to undischarged bankrupts, the 1963 Act prohibits them from becoming a director but the court can make exceptions.

The Companies Act 1990[12] brought in tough sanctions providing for Restriction Orders in relation to company directors who are found to have behaved dishonestly or irresponsibly.

Directors of insolvent companies – that is, companies who cannot pay their debts as they fall due – may be restricted by the court from acting as a director, company secretary or promoter of a company for a period of up to five years if they fail to satisfy the High Court that they

---

[10] S.45 of the Companies (Amendment) (No.2) Act 1999.

[11] Anomalously, a senile person may become a director in a Table A company but a person of unsound mind may not!

[12] S.150 of the Companies Act 1990.

have acted responsibly and honestly in their roles as company officers. The High Court will impose a restriction order if it is convinced that:

- the company continued to trade at a time when the director was aware that it was insolvent;

- the director was responsible for a breach of the requirements set out in the Companies Act in relation to the preservation of books of account and other company records;

- the director wilfully signed off on a statement of affairs which he knew to be inaccurate, unreliable or misleading; and

- the lifestyle of the director was supported financially by the company.

In relation to private companies, the capital requirement is €63,487 in allotted paid-up share capital. For public companies, the capital requirement is €317,435. Once a director of such a company is restricted, tougher rules apply in relation to capital maintenance.

Restrictions may also apply to shadow directors and to persons who have served as directors for a period of 12 months prior to the company being wound up. The High Court will not restrict a director if it is satisfied that:

- he has carried out his duties honestly and responsibly;

- he is a nominee of an institution, which has extended credit facilities to the company in question, once the directors have not given personal guarantees for such facilities. Such nominees must also persuade the court that they have acted honestly and responsibly; and

- he is merely a nominee of a venture capital company, which has bought or subscribed for shares in the company. Such nominees must also persuade the court that they have acted honestly and responsibly.

Restriction orders may be varied by the court. If it feels that the director in question has done nothing to convince the court that he will act in a more honest and responsible manner, the order can be extended. Conversely, the order will be lifted before the expiration of the five-year period if the court takes the view that the problems encountered in relation to the errant director have been remedied.

Disqualification orders, also provided for in the 1990 Act, are an even more severe measure of punishment and apply to "rogue directors" – those directors who have been convicted of fraud. A disqualification order prohibits a director from acting as a director, auditor, receiver, liquidator, examiner, promoter, manager or company officer for five years or for such other period as the Court deems appropriate.

The Registrar of Companies keeps a record of all restriction orders[13] and disqualification orders,[14] breaches of which are criminal offences and carry extremely serious penalties. These registers are available for inspection by members of the public. Details of all restriction orders and disqualification orders are also published by the Director of Corporate Enforcement on his website, www.odce.ie.

A person is automatically disqualified if he is:

- convicted on indictment of fraud, dishonesty,[15] or any indictable offence in relation to a company;

- gives a misleading or false statement or otherwise fails to notify to the CRO that he has been disqualified in another jurisdiction;[16]

- convicted of acting as a director while he is restricted and where statutory exceptions do not apply;

---

[13] S.153 of the Companies Act 1990.

[14] S.168 of the Companies Act 1990.

[15] S.160(1)(b) of the Companies Act 1990.

[16] S.42 of the Company Law Enforcement Act 2001, which amended s.160(1A) of the Companies Act 1990.

- convicted of acting as a director while under disqualification;

- convicted of acting as an auditor, liquidator, examiner, promoter or manager of a company while an undischarged bankrupt.

In addition to being disqualified, any person convicted of acting as a director while restricted is also guilty of a criminal offence and is liable to prosecution by the Director of Corporate Enforcement. The Court has *discretion* to disqualify a person from acting as a director when he has:

1. been convicted of fraud in relation to the company, shareholders or creditors;[17]

2. been found to be breach of duty in relation to the company's affairs;[18]

3. engaged in conduct unbecoming of a person charged with the management of a company, fraudulent or reckless trading resulting in the person being declared, personally liable for some or all of the company's debts;[19]

4. persistently defaulted in relation to his duties under the Companies Acts;[20]

5. failed to maintain proper books of account on two or more occasions;[21]

6. failed to file outstanding annual returns when asked to do so by the CRO;[22]

7. been disqualified in another jurisdiction or conduct in

---

[17] S.160(2)(a) of the Companies Act 1990.

[18] S.160(2)(b) of the Companies Act 1990.

[19] S.160(2))(c), (d) and (e) of the Companies Act 1990.

[20] S.160(2)(f) of the Companies Act 1990. Persistent default comprises three or more defaults over a period of five years.

[21] S.160(2)(g) Companies Act 1990.

[22] S.160(2)(h) of the Companies Act 1990.

another jurisdiction which would have resulted in disqualification in this jurisdiction,[23]

8.   been restricted as a director where the company of which he is a director is wound up within five years of the conduct prompting the restriction.[24]

Subject to statutory exceptions, any person who is found to be acting as a director of a company during a period in which he is restricted or disqualified may be held personally liable without any limitation for that company's debts if that company becomes insolvent during or within a period of one year of their having served as a director.[25]

The Phoenix Syndrome

The Phoenix Syndrome, the practice by which directors of insolvent companies leave large unpaid debts and set up similar businesses, was tackled by the 1990 Act.[26] Where a person has been a director of a company, which is insolvent and has been put into liquidation, the liquidator must report same to the Director of Corporate Enforcement. The Director of Corporate Enforcement has the discretion to relieve the liquidator of this duty. If the liquidator is not so relieved, the Director of Corporate Enforcement must bring an application to restrict the company director in question.

There are a number of exceptions. While the restriction applies only to companies, which are wound up after August 1, 1990, it covers persons who were directors and shadow directors within one year prior to the start of the liquidation process. It includes foreign registered companies which have businesses established in Ireland.

---

[23] S.160(2)(i) of the Companies Act 1990.

[24] S.160(5) of the Companies Act 1990.

[25] S.163(3) of the Companies Act 1990.

[26] Pt VII, Chap.1 of the Companies Act 1990, s.149.

Persons who are found to be in breach of restriction orders risk criminal prosecution.

RETIREMENT AND REMOVAL OF DIRECTORS

It is possible for directors to remain in office for the duration of their lives although most companies have in their Articles of Association provision for retirement. Equally, a company cannot prevent or penalise any of its directors from resigning.

Table A companies oblige all their directors to retire at the first AGM. Subsequently, one third of the directors must retire each year and on a rota basis. The directors who retire will be those who have longest office since their last election. Where directors are elected on the same day, the retirement shall be determined by the drawing of lots. Directors of Table A companies are deemed to have vacated their office if they are:

- found guilty of an indictable office;

- adjudged bankrupt;

- absent from board meetings without consent for six months,

- involved in arrangements with their creditors; or

- are of unsound mind.

Dismissal

Notwithstanding the circumstances set out above, there are no statutory grounds for the removal of a director from office. But in Table A companies, the members can pass a resolution removing any or all of the directors. And in other companies, Articles of Association often allow directors to remove fellow-members. Such regulations have been proven to be legally valid, even in cases where the removal was executed for reasons, which had nothing to do with the role of the director in question in the running of the company.

While the Acts may not set out the grounds for removal, section 182 of the 1963 Act represents one of the most important instruments at the disposal of shareholders, namely the right to remove by passing an ordinary resolution on a simple majority, any or all the directors from the board before the expiration of the terms of office.

The implications of this section are enormous. Ultimately, it gives to anyone who can influence 51% of the shareholders, the power to sack the board of directors and take over the company. This compares with a majority of 75%, which is required to change the Articles of Association.

Unless the Articles of Association make other provision, a notice period of 28 days is required to be given for the removal of a director. In the case where members of a company want to remove a director who has been appointed for life, a resolution must first be passed to change the Articles of Association.

Where a director is being removed, not only must the removal be provided for in the Articles and due notice be given, but members must be notified of all written representations and the director in question must be given the opportunity to address a meeting of the members. If the members proceed with the removal, they must compensate the director in accordance with his rights of under his contract of employment.

Section 182 is of such significance that it cannot be modified by a company's Articles of Association or by the provisions in any service contract. However, it may be fettered or undermined by agreements between groups of shareholders or between directors and groups of shareholders. An example of when this can happen is when compensation is paid to a director for loss of office. The Irish courts have yet to test whether section 182 can be weakened in this manner.

In extreme situations, the removal of a director can con-stitute "oppression" within the meaning of section 205 of the 1963 Act or indeed be grounds for liquidating the company. The director facing removal must demonstrate that he had a legitimate expectation to continue serving as a director. The example of the quasi-partnership may be appropriate to consider but the Irish courts have shown a reluctance to interfere with the rights of shareholders under section 182.

REMUNERATION, EXPENSES AND LOANS

The manner in which directors are remunerated is determined by the Articles of Association. A general meeting must be held to approve contracts of employment which cannot be broken by notice and which last over five years between a company and a director.

The Companies Acts do not specify how directors should be paid. They merely require that any payments be subject to income tax. The amount paid and the purpose and method of payment must be open to inspection by the shareholders. Remuneration may take different forms:

- emoluments or salaries that are taxable;
- expenses that are tax deductible for the company;
- dividends from shares;
- loans;
- "Golden Handshakes" or payments paid to directors on retirement; and
- pension payments.

Emoluments

Payments made by the board must be in accordance with the general fiduciary duty to act *bona fide* and in the interests of the company. Payments made by a general meeting may be challenged by any shareholder who believes that they might be a fraud on a minority of shareholders.

The Memorandum of Association or the Articles of Association must give express authority for the payment of fees to non-executive directors. In Table A companies, the general meeting has authority to determine such remuneration.

An executive director's right to payment from his company is based primarily on his contract. Where no contract exists, the right to payment may have to be implied on the principles of equity. Case law suggests that the right to payment as well as the terms and conditions, should be stipulated in the director's service contract.

Pensions

Employers may be obliged to pay pensions if they are part of a director's contract. Where the payment of the pension is not part of the contract and it brings no benefit on the company, it may be *ultra vires*. In several English cases, the payment of pensions to directors in seemingly gratuitous circumstances was allowed where provision was made in the company's objects clause.

Companies have an implied power to pay pensions to executive directors and to surviving members of their families who are classified as dependants. Table A companies are authorised to pay pensions to directors where the directors worked under a service contract in any capacity.

The payment of pensions is subject to taxation and details must be disclosed in the company's annual accounts

Golden Handshakes

These are payments made to directors over and beyond their normal pensions. It is not uncommon for these payments to be staggered over a period of years in order to avoid the requirement to pay tax. Tax is due if the payment is over €10,158 plus €761 per year of service.

Golden handshakes are subject to the approval of the members of the company at a general meeting and aggregate amounts must be disclosed in conjunction with the annual accounts. Only in exceptional circumstances can the payment of golden handshakes be considered unlawful. For instance, even if the correct procedures are followed, golden handshakes cannot be paid to directors in consideration of unpaid work in a company, which is going into liquidation.

Expenses, Loans and other Payments

All companies have an implied power to pay vouched expenses incurred by directors in the course of their work for the company. Table A companies have an express power to so do.

A loan paid to a director or security provided for such a loan may be impermissible, depending on the type of transactions and on the objects of the company. Also prohibited are loans from directors to themselves without the authority of the company's Articles of Association or without the approval of the shareholders. A director is in breach of his fiduciary duties if he fails to take appropriate action in circumstances where he is aware of such a transaction. Table A companies have no express authority to give loans or security for borrowings to directors or to their families.

The situation in relation to loans was severely restricted in Part III of the 1990 Act[27] which prohibited a company from making a loan or quasi-loan to a director of the same company or connected person. Prior to this piece of legislation, loans were often given to directors as tax efficient ways of paying them. Furthermore, they were commonly advanced at low interest rates and in many cases, they were not repaid.

Part III of the 1990 Act outlaws a range of transactions including loans, guarantees or security which have the effect of giving large credit at the company's expense to directors, their families, other connected persons and companies. This prohibition applies regardless of shareholder approval and a

---

[27] S.31 of the Companies Act 1990.

breach constitutes not only a civil wrong but also a criminal offence.

The transactions include loans, guarantees, securities, credit transactions and quasi-loans which are defined as arrangements whereby a third party pays money or reimburses expenditure incurred by a director or connected person on the basis that they will be compensated by the company. Credit transactions include leases, licences, hire purchase agreements, conditional sales in exchange for periodic payments of money, land, other goods and services on the understanding that the payment be postponed.

Not covered by this prohibition are expenses properly incurred in the course of work and loans in respect of which the director is not given preferential treatment over a comparable person outside the company. For instance, a director of a bank can take a loan from the bank as long as it is on the same terms as a loan given to a lay customer.

The borrower of a prohibited loan may have his loan voided. He is personally liable for all or part of the company's debts where the loan contributed significantly to its insolvency. He may also be the subject of a prosecution summarily or on indictment by the Director of Corporate Enforcement.

A company may avoid its obligations in relation to a prohibited transaction as long as:

- the money or property can be returned,

- the company has not been indemnified for any loss it sustained, and

- the rights of any third party purchaser are not prejudiced.

CHAPTER 6

Directors: Duties and Liabilities

INTRODUCTION

The obligations on a company director are many and in some instances onerous. Particularly in light of the change of approach heralded by the introduction of the Company Law Enforcement Act 2001, directors would be indeed foolish if they didn't acquaint themselves with the duties they bear and indeed the considerable powers they have.[1] In brief however, a different and more responsible role is contemplated for the company director under the new Act. But the Director of Corporate Enforcement is intent on helping company directors fulfil their legal obligations – not simply by strict enforcement of the law but by encouraging compliance in an atmosphere of co-operation.[2]

The members of a company, i.e. the people who actually own the company, operate through the instrument of the general meeting. The distinction between them and directors is that the latter group use the board of the company as the principal channel through which they fulfil their duties and use their powers.

Invariably, the members of a company delegate their pow-

---

[1] The statutory provisions which cover the role of directors are set out in ss.174–199 of the Companies Act 1963; Pts III, IV and VII of the Companies Act 1990; ss.43–45 of the Company Law (Amendment) (No. 2) Act 1999; and Pts 4 and 9 of the Company Law Enforcement Act 2001.

[2] S.12(1)(b) of the Company Law Enforcement Act 2001 states that the function of the Director of Corporate Enforcement shall be "to encourage compliance with the Companies Acts."

ers to their company's board of directors who manage the company on their behalf. If a simple majority of the company's members or shareholders sees fit, the directors can be removed from office. Directors should first examine their company's Articles of Association in order to properly understand their obligations.

In most instances, the board of directors of a small firm comprises a managing director, salaried executive directors, paid non-executive directors and a company secretary. In the case of bigger companies, sub-committees are given specific management functions. The degree to which directors may sub-contract their powers is a matter, which has yet to be resolved.

As long as companies fulfil the basic obligations set out in the Companies Acts, which require the appointment of at least two directors and a company secretary, companies may determine their own rules concerning the appointment and removal of directors.

For instance, in companies which have adopted the Articles of Association set out in Table A of the Companies Act 1963, directors have the power to manage the company's business. They have the general powers, which are delegated to them through the Articles of Association. If they exercise powers, which are not given to them in the Articles of Association, they are acting illegally or *ultra vires*, which literally means outside of their powers. Or if they purport to do an act, which the company does not have the power to do, the company – through the directors' actions – acts *ultra vires*.

Companies may even give to the managing director, specific powers to operate the company. It is the norm for directors to manage the company on a day-to-day basis but not first without adopting rules drawn up in consultation with the company's shareholders. In general, the shareholders' involvement is through the mechanism of the AGM or EGM. This line becomes somewhat blurred in the case of any Irish companies where the shareholders are also the directors of the company.[3]

Duties

Directors' duties – which are not unlike those of trustees – have their roots in common law, statute law, the company's own regulations and principles of equity. A director owes a fiduciary duty because he is the agent of the company. Legally speaking, he must behave in a manner, which is befitting the company, and he must place the interests of the company ahead of his own. The duty of a director of an insolvent company is primarily to act in the best interests of the creditors. He must also act in the interests of the company's employees although the employees cannot themselves enforce this interest. In common law, a director has duties:

- to exercise reasonable skill, care and diligence;

- to exercise authority including discretionary authority in the interests of the company;

- not to unjustly enrich himself from his role;

- to make a disclosure to the company where he derives material benefit from his role in the company or where he enters a contract with a shareholder, debtor or creditor;

- to avoid a conflict between his personal or economic interests and the interests of the company;

- to maintain proper systems of management in the company; and

- to attend as many board meetings as possible. He can use his absence as a defence when negligent decisions are taken without him.

Under the Companies Acts, a director has duties:

- to comply with his obligations under the Companies Acts.

---

[3] For the various types of Directors, see Chap.5 on *Directors: Appointment, Removal and Remuneration.*

Under the Company Law Enforcement Act 2001, a director will be presumed to have allowed a breach of the Acts unless he can prove that he took all reasonable measures to prevent such a breach.[4] This is a radical change because it represents a shift in the onus of proof. A director who is suspected of defaulting on his obligations will be presumed guilty until proven innocent. The onus is on the director to prove he has complied.

- to comply with his obligations to ensure that proper books of account are maintained.[5] This is becoming increasingly important in recent times; more than ever before, liquidators are making application for orders to deal with directors who do not fulfil their obligations in this regard.

Any director who does not take reasonable steps to ensure compliance is guilty of a criminal offence which can be tried summarily or – if it is more serious – on indictment.[6]

Where the failure to keep proper books of account is found to have contributed to the company's financial difficulties or to its liquidation, a guilty director will face the same penalty scale.[7] When these situations arise, a liquidator, creditor or contributory may apply to court for a declaration that such directors be held personally liable – and to an unlimited degree.[8]

- to prepare annual accounts, which must give "a true and fair view" of the company's affairs,[9]

---

[4] S.100 of the Company Law Enforcement Act 2001.

[5] See Chap.7 on *Auditors*.

[6] S.202 (10) of the Companies Act 1990.

[7] S.203(1) of the Companies Act 1990.

[8] S.204(1) of the Companies Act 1990.

[9] Although not legally defined, the phrase "true and fair view" denotes those financial statements, which have been prepared in accordance with the Companies Acts and in accordance with criteria set down by the Accounting Standards Board.

- to have the company's financial statements audited each year,[10]

- to comply with their obligations to keep various registers including a register of members, a register of debenture holders, minute books, a register of directors and secretaries, copies of directors' service contracts, register of directors' interests and register of secretary's interests.

This is not as onerous as it sounds. The contents of these registers comprise basic uncomplicated information, which – with the exception of minute books – needs to be updated only in occasional circumstances such as when a director retires or dies. That said, failure to fulfil these obligations is a criminal offence, which can be prosecuted summarily or on indictment.

- to ensure that certain documents are submitted to the Companies Registration Office. Among the documents which should be filed are the annual return, change of registered office, notice of an increase in nominal authorised capital, nomination of a new annual return date, notification of the creation of a charge or mortgage, memorandum of satisfaction of a charge, notice of the death of a company officer, change of director/secretary, ordinary resolutions and special resolutions.

Under a new provision,[11] the CRO can send out a notice to directors who have failed to deliver relevant documents. In this notice, a payment or fine is specified at a level commensurate with the default. Unless the problem is remedied within 21 days of receipt of the notice, the fine will be payable.

The Director of Corporate Enforcement can apply to the High Court for a declaration that a company officer be held

---

[10] For more on auditing, see Chap.7 on *Auditors*.

[11] S.66 of the Company Law Enforcement Act 2001.

personally liable on the basis of fraudulent trading or failure to keep proper books.[12] But once such an Order is made, creditors may apply for Orders regarding their entitlements in such a scenario.

Infringements of the regulations regarding the prompt filing of returns and other documents comprised approximately 80% of the problems encountered by auditors in the year 2002. These breaches were referred to the CRO, which in many instances successfully prosecuted offenders summarily in the District Court.

- to keep a register at the company's registered offices of all personal information regarding date of birth, nationality and address of directors along with information regarding other directorships held.[13]

Failure to keep such a register and to keep it updated or refusal to grant inspection of it will result in prosecution of directors. In addition, default fines of €63.50 will be imposed for each day on which the contravention continues.

- to disclose particulars concerning shares or debentures in all companies including related companies;[14]

- to disclose details of all payments made to him in connection with the transfer of shares in a company;[15]

- to keep directors' service contracts.[16] Service contracts include standard contractual terms. Most directors – unwisely – do not have them.

In addition to the normal fines, which can be handed down by the District and higher courts, default fines of €63.50 will

---

[12] S.251 of the Companies Act 1990.
[13] S.51(2) of the Companies Act 1990.
[14] S.53 of the Companies Act 1990.
[15] S.188 of the Companies Act 1963.
[16] S.50 of the Companies Act 1990.

be imposed for each day on which the contravention continues.

- to disclose to the other directors, any interest he has in a contract, transaction or arrangement – actual or proposed – in which the company is involved,[17]

- to convene an Annual General Meeting or an Extraordinary General Meeting as required.[18]

The Director of Corporate Enforcement, on the application of any member of the company, can direct that an AGM or EGM be held where he has reason to believe that the requirement to call such a meeting has not been observed. If a meeting is not held and if his direction is ignored, every director and company officer in default may be prosecuted.

- to get the approval by resolution of the company at a general meeting for any transactions regarding the acquisition by or sale to a director of any company assets exceeding €63,487 or 10% of the net assets of the company by reference to the accounts of the company for the last preceding year to have been laid before an AGM.[19]

Transactions made in contravention of this provision can, generally speaking, be rendered null and void. Furthermore, the directors involved and any connected persons or other directors who authorise such a transaction may be held liable to account to the company for any gain made – directly or indirectly. Equally, they may be held jointly and severally liable to indemnify the company for any loss or damage resulting from such a transaction.

---

[17] S.194 of the Companies Act 1963 as amended by s.47 of the Companies Act 1990.

[18] S.131 Companies Act of the 1963 as amended by s.14 of the Company Law Enforcement Act 2001. See also Chap.7 on *Meetings*.

[19] S.29 of the Companies Act 1990. This obligation also applies to connected parties who include near relatives, business partners and associated businesses.

A director, whether executive or non-executive, may be liable to the company for any foreseeable loss, which arises, from their negligence or ineptitude. Such directors may also be asked to resign from the board.

Where a prospectus is published prior to the issue of new shares, a director has a duty to subscribers to ensure that the information contained therein is accurate.

The Director of Corporate Enforcement may apply to the High Court for an injunction under section 371 of the Companies Act 1963.[20] Such an injunction, which previously was capable of being sought by the CRO, obliges a director or a company to comply with their duties or make good their default under the Companies Acts. The costs of these applications are borne by the respondent director or the company involved, unless they can show good reason.

This new feature will be of particular use in relation to compliance with the filing obligations and the new Annual Return Date. The Director of Corporate Enforcement merely has to serve a 14-day notice on the respondent. What normally happens is that compliance is forthcoming during that period and the applications are simply struck out, but there have already been many instances where the injunctions are granted at significant cost to the respondents.

Restriction and Disqualification[21]

In any case, the Director of Corporate Enforcement, a liquidator or receiver may apply for an order restricting persons who were directors or company officer over the preceding 12 months from having any association with a company for a period of up to five years if he feels that that person has failed to act honestly and responsibly in relation to the conduct of that company's affairs.[22]

---

[20] S.96 of the Company Law Enforcement Act 2001.

[21] For more on this issue, see chap.5 on *Directors: Appointment, Removal and Remuneration.*

[22] S.150 of the Companies Act 1990 as amended by s.41 of the

This is one of the most important changes introduced by the Company Law Enforcement Act 2001 because before its enactment, only on rare occasions did a voluntary liquidator bring such an application. A liquidator used to be merely *permitted* to bring such an application. Now he is *legally obliged* – unless he is specifically relieved by the Director of Corporate Enforcement.

Auditors

On request, directors must provide information to auditors. Directors are obliged to provide auditors with "such information and explanations that are within their knowledge or can be procured by them as [are] necessary for the performance of the duties of the auditors."

Failure to produce the information is a criminal offence, which can be prosecuted by the Director of Corporate Enforcement. It is also an offence to give information, which is knowingly or recklessly false, deceptive or misleading.

If they are convicted of any indictable criminal offence under the Companies Acts, the Director of Corporate Enforcement can apply to court for an order disqualifying them to act as a director, other officer, receiver, liquidator or examiner for periods determined by the court. Such application can be made at any time within five years after conviction on indictment.[23] A director or company officer may also be disqualified if he fails to notify the CRO of his cessation as a director or secretary.

A director of a company, which is insolvent, can be charged with a criminal offence if he is found to have

---

Company Law Enforcement Act 2001. Restriction is limited to companies where the nominal allotted share capital of a public limited company shall be at least €317,434. In the case of any other company, the allotted share capital shall be €63,487.

[23] S.160 of the Companies Act 1990 as amended by s.42 of the Company Law Enforcement Act 2001.

misapplied or wrongfully retained or become liable or responsible for money of property belonging to the company. It is also an offence to have wrongfully exercised lawful authority or to breach the trust, which has been placed in him. The Director of Corporate Enforcement has the power to initiate such a prosecution.

Reckless trading is defined as the carrying on of business, which a director ought to have known, would result in the loss of creditors' money or the company's money. Reckless trading is also deemed to have existed if a director was party to the taking out of a loan on behalf of the company, which he knew could not be repaid.

The Director of Corporate Enforcement can bring a civil action against the director if it is suspected that he is liable for the company's debts and that those debts arise out of reckless trading.[24] But fraudulent trading is a criminal offence and can lead to unlimited personal liability, fines of up to €63,000 and seven-year terms of imprisonment.

A majority of directors of companies, which seek to go into members' voluntary liquidation, are obliged to make an accurate declaration of solvency.[25] This declaration must be accompanied by a report from an independent qualified person who must concur with the accuracy of the solvency declaration. If this declaration is not made, then the liquidation must continue as a creditors' voluntary liquidation. A director can be held personally liable for all of the company's debts if the declaration has been deliberately falsified.[26]

Where the Director of Corporate Enforcement has reason to suspect that a company director has not fulfilled his duties in this regard, he will firstly try to secure compliance. If unsuccessful, he can initiate a prosecution.

---

[24] S.297A of the Companies Act 1963 as inserted by s.138 of the Companies Act 1990.

[25] S.256 of the Companies Act 1963, as amended by s.128 of the Companies Act 1990.

[26] S.256(8) of the Companies Act 1963.

Standard of Care

There is no fixed standard of care for directors but it must be commensurate with the quality of experience. A more exacting standard of care will be required of a director who has been a senior accountant for many years than from say, an 18-year-old athlete who is a director of a sports' guarantee company.

Where a complaint of negligence has been made against a director, it is the company, which is able to sue him for damages. A shareholder or a liquidator cannot sue unless there is a breach of trust. However, any clause in the company's rules or in the director's service contract, which seeks to indemnify him from liability in negligence, is invalid.

Fiduciary Duties

These are the set of duties, which are generally common to the relationship that exists between directors and their company; trustees and trust beneficiaries; partners and each other; and solicitors and their clients. A fiduciary is obliged to act fairly on behalf of his company and is not allowed to act out his own selfish interests or in the interests of connected third parties. He must act in the interests of all the members, which comprise the company – and not just a section of the members or indeed himself.

Where an insolvent company is concerned, the director must act in the interests of the creditors and not exclusively the members or the employees. But the interests of creditors, members and employees may often be similar.

Where the interests of the company and the interests of employees clash, the director's duty is to the company.[27]

---

[27] S.52 of the Companies Act 1990.

ABUSE OF POWER

Fiduciaries must act in the interests of the company. But particularly in larger companies, it is often difficult to determine what the members' best interests are. For this reason, the courts tend to intervene only when directors are considered to have acted in a blatantly unfair manner towards a certain group of shareholders.

Fettering Discretion

Fiduciaries must not enter into promises or agreements with outside agents or with groups of shareholders, which have the effect, or intention of restricting the manner in which they exercise their discretion. It is difficult to determine what constitutes a fettering of discretion. Agreements for instance, which require a company's directors to act in a certain manner in return for an allotment of shares may not constitute a fettering of discretion if it can be shown that the greater interests of the company are being served by following such a course.

Advancing Own Interests

While a director is in breach of his fiduciary duties if he acts in a manner that merely furthers his own personal interests, it is difficult to prove. Frequently, a director's own interests and those of the company will be the same. But the courts will thoroughly investigate the motives of directors involved in alleged self-dealing.

Advancing the Interests of Third Parties

This is difficult to prove but directors will be found to be in breach of their fiduciary duties if for example, they give generous gifts to third parties in circumstances where such gestures cannot be explained as being in the best interests of the company. Gifts, which are regarded as "non-advanta-geous," may be considered as acts of oppression of or fraud on a minority.

The 1990 Act included a provision, which stated that in the performance of his functions, a director should have regard to the interests of the company's employees in general as well as the interests of its members. But this duty can be enforced only by the company and not by the employees.

Issuing Shares

Directors are in breach of the 1983 Companies (Amendment) Act and of their fiduciary duties if they allot shares with the intention of blocking a take-over or changing the voting strengths in a company – instead of seeking to raise more capital. Regarding the allotment of shares,

- Directors can only exercise such power if authorised by the company in a general meeting or by the Articles of Association.
- The maximum number of shares to be allotted and the date before which they are to be allotted must be stated.
- Powers of allotment must be exercised *bona fide* and in the best interests of the company.
- Directors must observe the statutory pre-emption rights of existing shareholders – or rights of first refusal – in accordance with the size of their shareholding.
- A period of 21 days is allowed to existing shareholders to consider their pre-emption rights.
- Directors who breach the share allotment provisions of the 1983 Act will make the company and every officer who knowingly authorised or allowed the breach, jointly and severally liable to compensate the person would should have been offered shares.

If compliance cannot be secured out of court, the Director of Corporate Enforcement can bring a prosecution against errant directors either summarily or on indictment.

Conflicts of Interest

Directors can be convicted of fraud or conspiracy to defraud if they unjustly enrich themselves at the expense of their company. They must at all times ensure that they do not put themselves in situations where their own interests and those of the company are in conflict.

Equally, a director may not use company property for his own benefit unless he has the permission of the shareholders. The word 'property' can have a broad definition; it may be construed in such a way as to include confidential information.

Unless it is expressly prohibited in the service contract or elsewhere, a director may participate in a competing company. A partner is not allowed to participate in a competing business unless he has the permission of the other partners.

A director is in breach of his fiduciary duty if he intercepts for his own personal gain, business that should properly belong to the company of which he is a director. A director may have to turn the profit from corporate opportunities over to the company even if he makes full disclosure and the company is not interested.

If he fails to comply with the requests of the Director of Corporate Enforcement, he can be prosecuted summarily or on indictment.

Property Transactions

If persons who have been directors want to purchase any of the company's substantial assets from the receiver or liquidator, 14 days notice must be given by the receiver or liquidator to all creditors of his intention to sell to the directors.

Directors are required to obtain shareholder approval in respect of the purchase or sale of substantial non-cash assets of the company of requisite value. Requisite value covers assets worth more than €63,500 or 10% of the company's relevant assets by reference to the company's most recent balance sheet.[28]

In reality, such transactions are fraught with difficulty. All transactions and transfer deeds must be accompanied by certificates of compliance with section 29 of the 1990 Act issued by the CRO. Failure to get section 29 approval leads to the voiding of the transaction. Any gain made by the director must be paid to the company. Alternatively, he must compensate the company for any loss suffered.

Internal Contracts

A director has a fiduciary duty not to enter into a contract with his own company. In the landmark 1854 case of *Aberdeen Railway Company v. Blaikie Bros*,[29] the House of Lords ruled that contracts of this kind are voidable on the initiative of the company. Furthermore, unless the Articles of Association so permit, a director cannot vote and cannot be counted in the quorum at meetings held to consider contracts in which he has an interest.

This rule is often relaxed by a company's Articles of Association, which can permit a director to enter into contracts with his company as long as he makes full disclosure at a general meeting. Directors of Table A companies avail of Article 83, which requires full disclosure of the nature of the interest in accordance with section 194 of the 1990 Act.

Section 194 obliges a director to disclose at a meeting of the directors any direct or indirect interest in contracts or proposed contracts. The section does not require the directors to approve the interest.

---

[28] This provision, contained in s.29 of the 1990 Act, applies to shadow directors and persons connected to the director.

[29] (1854) 1 Macq. 61.

Insider Dealing

Insider Dealing cannot be regarded as a fraud on the company for the purposes of litigation because the company may not suffer any real loss as a result of dealings in its securities. The determination of the House of Lords in the 1902 case of *Percival v. Wright*[30] still has authority. The shareholders' rights under the Articles of Association do not extend to rights against the directors when dealing in the company's shares. But an aggrieved shareholder will succeed at law where the information received by the insider was misleading or was intended to engage him in the transaction.

A director is prohibited from dealing in options in his company's shares because of the inherent potential for lucrative profits. Shares must be listed on the Stock Exchange. The prohibition extends to shadow directors and applies to options in debentures. It does not apply to the purchase of convertible debentures or to the purchase of options to subscribe to securities.

Insider dealing is a criminal offence and defined in section 108 of the 1990 Act as the dealing in the company's shares, debentures or other debt securities by persons who are connected with the company and are in possession of confidential sensitive information. Insiders include anyone who, within the preceding six months, was a

- director,
- shadow director,
- secretary,
- employee,
- auditor,
- liquidator,
- receiver,

---

[30] [1902] 2 Ch. 421.

- examiner,

- person administering a compromise or scheme with creditors,

- shareholder,

- officer of a substantial shareholder,

- person who because of a professional, business or other relationship with the company, would reasonably be expected to have access to sensitive confidential information, or

- 'tipee' – person who comes into possession of sensitive information from any of the above types of persona and who should know they are not allowed to use the information for share dealing.

This list extends to the same categories of person who have such relationships with related companies, be they subsidiaries or holding companies. Actions for breach of these provisions must be brought within a two-year period. The plaintiff can claim compensation for any loss incurred and any profits made must be accounted for.

If the Court concludes that a director has engaged in insider dealing, affected parties can prosecute compensation claims. The Director of Corporate Enforcement can initiate a prosecution, which can lead to the imposition on guilty directors and company officers of fines of up to €254,000. In addition or as an alternative, a jail sentence of up to ten years may be imposed.

Disclosure of Interests

The directors and secretary of a company are, under the Companies Act 1963 Act, required to disclose in a company share register all the shares, and debentures they have in that company. This obligation covers members of their families and shares held in trust. These interests are notifiable to allow other shareholders to know what stake the directors have. They must register their ownership of any interest within four days of the date of awareness of the interest. The register of interests includes a full record of all the company's shares and debentures, which are held by the directors and the secretary. It can be inspected free of charge by any member of the company.

Failure to register such details can result in a prosecution being brought summarily or on indictment by the Director of Corporate Enforcement.

Cheques and Orders

In relation to company business, directors will be personally liable for the amount cited on cheques, money orders and bills of exchange on which the company's name is not properly identified in legible letters. Liability can arise when the words "Limited," "Ltd", "Teoranta" or "Teo" are absent from the company name as it appears.

Distribution of Profits

Directors are liable to the company if they distribute profits, which are not authorised. The company must be solvent before the distribution of profits can be authorised.

CHAPTER 7

Auditors

INTRODUCTION

Arguably the most significant aspect of the Company Law Enforcement Act 2001 relates to the changed role and duties of auditors. With some exceptions, which are discussed below, every company incorporated in the State must have an audit of its books carried out each year. When an audit is carried out, a company's financial statements and books of account are closely scrutinised by an auditor to ensure that they provide a "true and fair view" of the companies business and that the records have been kept in accordance with the requirements of the Companies Acts.

Auditors are obliged to report any suspected failure to maintain proper books of account to the CRO.[1] Under the new legislation, the CRO must then notify the Director of Corporate Law Enforcement.[2] Auditors may be obliged to hand over all relevant information with the view to preparing a prosecution under the Companies Acts. They must also submit a report to the Director of Corporate Law Enforcement setting out their reasons for believing that the company in question has committed an offence under the Companies Acts.

It represents a radical change in the culture and operation of company culture in Ireland. The auditor, regarded by many in years gone by as a personage who assists the company in maintaining good records, is regarded unfairly by some directors as a whistle-blower! It is more fair to describe him as a person who is just one of a number of agents participating

---

[1] S.194(1)(b) of the Companies Act 1990.
[2] S.74(b) of the Company Law Enforcement Act 2001.

in the effort to secure greater compliance – and ultimately a better business environment.

That said, if he is not satisfied with the presentation and content of the company's accounts, he will in the first instance find out whether the company can remedy breaches he has uncovered. But if the co-operation of the company cannot be secured, he can bring the company to the notice of the CRO and the Office of the Director of Corporate Enforcement. In serious cases, this can ultimately have the effect of subjecting the company and its directors to criminal prosecution.

The Companies (Auditing and Accounting) Bill 2003 which is due to be enacted by the Oireachtas later this year contains significant changes to the manner in which auditors conduct their business.[3]

Among the most important developments is the establishment of the Irish Auditing and Accounting Supervisory Authority, to be known as the IAASA. It will be funded jointly by the Government and by the various accountancy bodies. When the Bill becomes law, the remit of auditors – currently derived from the accountancy bodies – will be transferred by ministerial order to the IAASA.

The function of the IAASA will be to work with the accountancy bodies in developing professional accounting and auditing standards and take action when auditors and accountants fail to comply with these standards. It is intended that the new Supervisory Authority will monitor the effectiveness of the rules relating to the independence of auditors and the disciplinary procedures of accountancy bodies. The remainder of this chapter is written on the basis of the legislation as it currently stands.

---

[3] This Bill was introduced on foot of the Report of the Review Group on Auditing, which was itself established in the aftermath of the DIRT Inquiry. Copies of the Bill are available from the Government Publications Office, Molesworth Street, Dublin 2.

QUALIFICATIONS OF AN AUDITOR [4]

An auditor must be a member of a recognised body of accountants.[5] Furthermore, he must have a valid practising certificate from one of the recognised bodies. The Minister for Enterprise, Trade and Employment can also authorise persons to act as auditors.[6]

In the Companies (Auditing and Accounting) Bill 2003, it is proposed that the CRO maintain a Register of Auditors.[7]

If a person acts as an auditor or holds himself out as an auditor and is not listed on the Register of Auditors, he is committing a criminal offence punishable by a fine not exceeding €2,000 if convicted summarily. Daily default fines of up to €60 may be imposed for continued contravention. If convicted on indictment, the maximum penalty is €12,500 with a daily default fine of not more than €300.[8]

Parties or companies who have associations with companies being audited – including company officers, employees and undischarged bankrupts – are precluded from acting as auditors. Those who have not upheld the Code of Ethics of their respective bodies may initially find themselves the sub-

---

[4] For more information on the proposed amendment regarding the qualification of auditors, see s.34 of the Companies (Auditing and Accounting) Bill 2003.

[5] S.191 of the Companies Act 1990 gives recognition to the following institutions, of which persons must be members in order to act as auditors:
- The Institute of Chartered Accountants in Ireland;
- The Association of Chartered Certified Accountants;
- The Institute of Chartered Accountants in England and Wales;
- The Institute of Chartered Accountant in Scotland;
- The Institute of Incorporated Public Accountants; and
- The Institute of Certified Public Accountants in Ireland.

[6] S.199(3) of the Companies Act 1990 validates the appointment of those persons as auditors who obtained ministerial authorisation before February 3, 1983.

[7] S.36 of the Companies (Auditing and Accounting) Bill 2003.

[8] S.36(4) of the Companies (Auditing and Accounting) Bill 2003.

ject of disciplinary actions, which may eventually lead to disqualification.

WHAT IS AN AUDIT?

An audit is an independent examination of a company's financial statements. It is conducted by an auditor whose objective is to give the members of the company an informed, independent and professional assessment of the financial statements put together by the company's directors. The aim of the exercise is to give an assurance to the company's members that they have been given a true and fair view of the state of the company at any given point in time. The members of a company also want to be told that the financial statements – and in particular its profit and loss account – have been prepared in accordance with standard accounting practice and with their obligations under the Companies Acts.

In addition auditors – in performing audits – must comply with the standards set by the Auditing Practices Board. In conducting an audit, auditors must:

- Analyse the overall presentation of the financial statements so that they can come decide if they have been prepared in accordance with acceptable accounting standards and the Companies Acts;

- carry out procedures to extract the evidence required to ascertain whether the financial statements give a fair and accurate view; and

- issue to the company members a report in which they give their view on the quality of the financial statements supplied.

ROLE OF AN AUDITOR

On the formation of the company, the directors can themselves appoint their first auditor. Alternatively, the auditor can be appointed at a general meeting of the company. Subsequently, the auditor is appointed at the AGM of the company by the members. The auditor stays in office until the next AGM.

On setting about his work, the auditor supplies the company with a "letter of engagement." This outlines the respective responsibilities of the auditor and the directors. The auditor is supposed have knowledge of the industry in which the company operates. This enables him to decide which aspects of the financial statements are more likely to present a risk of misstatement. Once this is done, the following questions must be addressed by the auditor:

- Has the company maintained proper books of account?[9]

- Have books of account from all branches of the company been examined?

- Do the financial statements give a true and fair view of the company's business?

- Are the judgments and estimates of the directors accurate?

- Have tests supported the figures contained in the financial statements?

- Have the financial statements have been prepared in accordance with the Companies Acts?

- Are there internal controls? If so, are they effective?

- How strong are the internal controls employed by company management?

- How co-operative was the company in the preparation of the audit?

---

[9] S.202 of the Companies Act 1990 requires the books of account to contain a record of all goods bought and sold by the company, to represent a true and fair view of the financial condition of the company, to include a statement regarding the company's stocks at the end of the year and to contain a record of the assets and liabilities held by the company.

- Is there a legal requirement to hold an EGM?

- Is the directors' report consistent with the financial statements?

- Do the books of account support the view contained in the company's balance sheet?

- Was all necessary information forthcoming from the company?

- Have the accounting policies been reasonable, have they been properly explained and have they disclosed all the relevant information?

- Did anything happen in the post-balance sheet period that might be likely to have a material effect on the financial statement?

The auditor must then issue the members of the company with his report.

COMPANIES EXEMPTED FROM CARRYING OUT AN AUDIT

The general rule is that every company must have their accounts audited once a year. But a company is exempt from carrying out an audit in circumstances limited by law.[10] In the current situation, the main conditions for audit exemption are as follows:

1. company turnover must not exceed €317,435 in a year;

2. the total on the balance sheet must not be greater than €1,905 million;

3. the average number of staff must be under 50;

4. the company does not own a subsidiary, and

---

[10] Pt III of the Companies (Amendment) (No. 2) Act 1999. In the Companies (Auditing and Accounting) Bill 2003, it is proposed to increase the exemption threshold.

5. the company has fulfilled its obligations regarding the filing of documents to the CRO.

Even where a company is exempt, it remains obliged to keep proper books of account.

DUTIES OF AN AUDITOR

The auditor's main duty is to report to the company members on the financial statements.[11] In his report, he must state whether the company has kept proper books of account, whether the financial statements have been prepared in accordance with the provisions of the Companies Act and whether they give a true and fair view of the company's profit and loss account. The auditor must give his opinion of the directors' report and whether it is consistent with the information he has examined.

The auditor must also state whether he has been given access to all the information he requires for the purposes of an audit and whether the balance sheet is consistent with the books of account.

The auditor is legally obliged to reveal details concerning payments to directors including salaries, fees, expenses and pension contributions – even where this information does not appear in the information contained in the financial statements.

Where the auditor cannot report a satisfactory state of affairs, he must "qualify" his audit report. There are two forms qualification. He can:

> enter a **disclaimer of opinion**. In other words, he can state that he cannot come to a view on whether the financial statements give a true and fair view. This may be done where there has been a limitation on the scope of the audit.

---

[11] S.193(1) of the Companies Act 1990.

or

enter an **adverse opinion**. By this, it is meant that the auditors state unequivocally that the financial statements do not give a true and fair view of the company's financial situation. This may be necessary when the auditor disagrees with the directors' report.

The auditor has a duty to report to the Company Registration Office where a company has failed to maintain proper books of account.[12] He must serve notice on the company in the first instance and if corrective measures are not taken within one week, he must notify the CRO, which in turn informs the Director of Corporate Enforcement.

The auditor must report any information to the Director of Corporate Enforcement, which leads him to the view that an indictable offence has been committed by the company or by an officer or agent of the company.[13] He must give a full explanation for his opinion. To assist the auditor in complying with this obligation, he may rely on the guidance, which has been published jointly by the Office of the Director of Corporate Enforcement, the Auditing Practices Board and the Consultative Committee of Accountancy Bodies Ireland.[14]

The auditor has an obligation to carry out his task with professional integrity.[15] He must exercise due skill and care. He cannot exclude liability and he cannot get the company to indemnify him against liability to third parties. If an auditor is negligent in this regard, he may be sued for damages by

---

[12] S.194 of the Companies Act 1990 as amended by s.74 of the Company Law Enforcement Act 2001.

[13] S.194(5) of the Companies Act 1990 as inserted by s.74 of the Company Law Enforcement Act 2001.

[14] These guidelines are available on the Director of Corporate Enforcement's website, the address of which is www.odce.ie.

[15] S.193(6) of the Companies Act 1990.

the company or by other parties such as the members, shareholders or would-be shareholders.

If requested, the auditor must supply evidence of his qualifications to the Director of Corporate Enforcement.[16]

Failure on the part of the auditor to fulfil his duties under the Companies Acts can result in penal sanctions. If his negligence is found to have contributed to the insolvency of the company or to have otherwise damaged the company, he can be sued. Equally, he can be prosecuted if he wrongfully certifies that the company's accounts represent a true and fair view of the company's financial state. Depending on the seriousness of the breach of duty, he may be found guilty on indictment an can be fined as much as €12,700 and/or be imprisoned for up to five years. If convicted summarily, the penalty can be as high as €1,900 and/or 12 months in jail.

RIGHTS OF AN AUDITOR

The auditor is entitled to be paid.[17] If he is appointed by the directors, the terms and conditions are determined by the directors. Otherwise, details of his remuneration are decided by the company at its AGM

An auditor may have access to the company's books, accounts and vouchers at all reasonable times.[18] The officers and employees of the company are required to give him all the information he believes is necessary for him to perform his duties.[19] This obligation also applies to officers and employees of subsidiary companies incorporated within the state. The company must take all reasonable steps to get the

---

[16] S.187(12)(a) of the Companies Act 1990 as inserted by s.72 of the Company Law Enforcement Act 2001.

[17] S.160 of the Companies Act 1963 as amended by s.183 of the Companies Act 1990.

[18] S.193 of the Companies Act 1990.

[19] S.197(3) of the Companies Act 1990.

required co-operation of its subsidiaries, which are outside the state.

An officer or employee who fails to fulfil his duties in relation to an auditor is guilty of an offence under the Companies Acts. If convicted summarily, a fine of up to €1,900 can be imposed along with or instead of a jail term of 12 months. A jail term of up to five-years and/or a fine of up to €12,700 can be handed down if the conviction is on indictment.

An auditor has the right to attend any meeting of the company.[20] He must receive the same notices and communications as do the members. Auditors have the right of audience at all such meetings.

An auditor has a right to oppose attempts to remove him from office by resolution at a general meeting or by resolution appointing a replacement.[21]

An auditor is allowed to resign from office before the expiry of his term of office. He must give written notice to the company and the CRO. In this notice, the auditor must state why he is resigning. The Minister for Enterprise, Trade and Employment will appoint a replacement auditor in situations where within a week of such a resignation, the company has put no replacement in place.

---

[20] S.161 of the Companies Act 1963 as amended by s.184 of the Companies Act 1990.

[21] S.161 of the Companies Act 1963 as amended by s.184 of the Companies Act 1990.

CHAPTER 8

Examiners

The purpose of an examinership is to try to rescue ailing companies where there is a reasonable prospect of survival and thereby of saving jobs and maximising the return for creditors.

An examiner can be appointed for a period of 70 days.[1] The court can grant an extension of 30 days. During this period, the company is placed under the "protection" of the court, and it is insulated from pressure being applied by creditors.

If the examiner believes the company is capable of being rescued, he prepares a survival plan known as the "Scheme of Arrangement" to facilitate the company's continued existence.

If the liabilities of the company are less than €317,435, the case can be transferred from the High Court to the Circuit Court, thus saving the company costs. The grounds for the appointment of an examiner are as follows:

1. the company cannot and is unlikely to pay its debts as they fall due and its assets are of less value than its liabilities, including contingent and prospective liabilities;

2. no winding up or liquidation order has been made;

3. the appointment of an examiner would offer the company – or any part of it – a reasonable prospect of survival;[2] and

---

[1] S.5 of the Companies Act 1990 as amended by s.14 of the Companies (Amendment) (No. 2) Act 1999.

[2] S.2 of the Companies (Amendment) Act 1990 as amended by s.181(1)(a) of the Companies Act 1990 and s.5 of the Companies (Amendment) (No. 2) Act 1999.

4. an examiner may not be appointed in circumstances where a receiver has been appointed for three days.

Application for the appointment of an examiner is made *ex parte*, i.e. there is no requirement to give notice to any other party. Who can apply?

- The company – through an ordinary resolution passed by its members.

- A simple majority of the directors. This is the most common source of applications.

- Creditors – including contingent and prospective creditors and also employees.

- Member or members holding at least 10% of the issued share capital.

The application or petition must however be made in good faith and it must be based on information which is factually correct.[3] The petition must be accompanied by a report from an independent accountant – either the company's auditor or someone who is qualified to be appointed as the examiner. This report should include all relevant details of the company and should assess the prospects for the company's return to a healthy financial state. It is also required to recommend a particular course of action including details of arrangements with creditors.[4]

The person who is willing to be appointed as the Examiner should exhibit his consent in writing. In circumstances where the petitioner – for reasons, which could not have been foreseen – cannot supply a report from an independent ac-

---

[3] S.3 of the Companies (Amendment) Act 1990 as amended by s.180(1)(a) of the Companies Act 1990 and ss.6, 7 and 8 of the Companies (Amendment)(No. 2) Act 1999.

[4] S.3(3A) and s.3(3B) of the Companies (Amendment) Act 1990 as inserted by s.7 of the Companies (Amendment) (No. 2) Act 1999.

countant in support of his petition, the company can be placed under the protection of the court for a limit of up to ten days.[5]

The petition must be advertised after it has been presented and before it has been heard by the court. The purpose is to give every creditor the chance to express an opinion. Only then can the court appoint an examiner.[6] Before the court can appoint an examiner, it must be convinced that there is a reasonable chance that the company can survive with the help of the Scheme of Arrangement.

QUALIFICATIONS OF AN EXAMINER

There are no precise requirements, but in normal circumstances the examiner is a practising accountant. Persons precluded from being examiners include:

• persons who are not eligible to act as a liquidator in the company in question;[7]

• corporate bodies, undischarged bankrupts and persons otherwise connected with the company; and

• persons who have been disqualified from acting as an examiner to any company.

CONSEQUENCES OF EXAMINERSHIP

• The protection begins from the date of the petition – not the date of the court order appointing the examiner – and it lasts for 70 days.

• The title of the company changes to X Ltd in Examination (under the Companies (Amendment) Act 1990).

---

[5] S.3A of the Companies (Amendment) Act 1990 as inserted by s.9 of the Companies (Amendment) (No. 2) Act 1999.

[6] S.3(B) of the Companies (Amendment) Act 1990 as inserted by s.10 of the Companies (Amendment) (No. 2) Act 1999.

[7] S.28 of the Companies (Amendment) Act 1990.

- Creditors are prohibited from taking any action against the company, which could have the effect of reducing its asset value.

- Ordinary creditors do not have the right to petition the court to have the company wound up. Neither can they seek to enforce a judgment against the company.

- Secured creditors will not be permitted to enforce charges over part or all the company's property unless the examiner consents.

- A receiver cannot be appointed. The receiver must cease if he has been appointed within a period of three days before the appointment of the examiner. If he has been appointed outside that period, his work can be restricted by the court.

- With the approval of the court, an examiner can ignore negative pledge clauses in debentures so as to borrow the necessary funds for the period of the protection.

- If it thinks it is fair and equitable, the court can restrict the role of directors or it can transfer their powers to the examiner. If the directors are restricted, the examiner can sell the company's assets if he thinks it can help the rescue of the company. If any such assets are the subject of a charge or mortgage, the holder of the security retains the same priority in respect of payment.[8]

- A shareholder cannot bring an action claiming oppression of a minority[9] in relation to issues, which arise during the period of protection.

- No other legal proceedings can be brought against the company without the permission of the court.

- Guarantors and sureties may be asked to pay money but proceedings cannot be brought against them.

---

[8] S.11(3) of the Companies Act 1990 as amended by s.181 of the Companies (Amendment) (No. 2) Act 1999.

[9] S.205 of the Companies Act 1963.

- If adopted by the court, the examiner's Scheme of Arrangement is binding on all persons and groups who are liable for the company's debts.

DUTIES OF AN EXAMINER

The examiner must

- report to the court within 35 days of his appointment as to whether he has been able to formulate proposals for a Scheme of Arrangement. The document comprises a series of detailed coherent proposals as to how the company can return to a position of financial strength;

- ensure that the Scheme of Arrangement specifies different classes of members and creditors and makes sure that the interests of various groups are equally treated;

- send out his Scheme of Arrangement to the different classes of members and creditors, including a statement, which explains the implications of the proposals;

- if the examiner cannot draw up such an arrangement within this period, he must go to court and seek directions, which might include an order for the company to be wound up;

- report on fraudulent and reckless transactions he encounters in the course of the company's business;

- compile a report for the assistance of the court in the event of the court calling a hearing to consider allegations made by the independent accountant concerning fraud or misappropriation of company property;[10]

- carry out any other duties, which are ordered by the court;[11] and

- act in good faith.[12]

---

[10] S.13A of the Companies (Amendment) Act 1999 as inserted by s.21 of the Companies (Amendment) (No. 2) Act 1999.

[11] S.15(2) of the Companies (Amendment) Act 1990.

[12] S.4 of the Companies Act 1990 as amended by S.13 of the Companies (Amendment) (No. 2) Act 1999.

If the examiner fails to fulfil his duties in relation to the company under the protection of the court, he shall be guilty of an offence, which is punishable by a fine of up to €1,900 and/or one-year imprisonment if tried summarily. The fine can be as high as €12,700 and/or five years imprisonment if he is convicted on indictment.

POWERS OF AN EXAMINER

The examiner can

- have access at all reasonable times to the company's books, vouchers and accounts.[13] Furthermore, he can expect the co-operation of all company officers and agents. They are legally obliged to give him any relevant documents and to give sworn evidence. This requirement covers all companies incorporated within the State, which are subsidiaries of the company in examination. The company is obliged to supply information to the examiner regarding subsidiaries, which are incorporated, outside the State;

- convene meetings of directors, set the agenda, propose resolutions and present reports;[14]

- seek the direction of the court at any time;

- appoint a committee comprising creditors. This committee can be convened at any time to give advice;[15]

- apply to the court to have the powers of the directors transferred to him. If successful, the examiner can vet all contracts entered into by the company and third parties;

- **the examiner may be held personally liable for contracts entered into in the company's name or in his own name. But he may be reimbursed from the assets of the**

---

[13] S.7 of the Companies (Amendment) Act 1990.

[14] S.7(3) of the Companies (Amendment) Act 1990 as amended by s.18 of the Companies (Amendment) (No. 2) Act 1999.

[15] S.21 of the Companies (Amendment) Act 1990.

company if the court gives permission.[16] **This liability will not attach if there is a stipulation to the contrary**;

- sell property over which there is a floating charge. The charge transfers to the property, which replaced the property, originally charged;

- take any action he believes is needed in order to stop activity or resolve problems created by activity which he thinks is not in the best interests of the company. He may not repudiate contracts entered into prior to his appointment;[17]

- bring a prosecution against directors, shadow directors, company officers or connected persons for fraudulent or reckless trading.[18] Such persons may be found guilty of a criminal offence and may be held personally liable – even if it can be proven that they were knowingly party or should have known that they were party to activity, which had as its intention the defrauding of creditors;

- borrow money when the directors' powers have been transferred to him by the court. As the examiner will find it difficult to borrow money, additional expenditure will be regarded as expenses and thus will have priority in payment;

- apply to the High Court for an order directing the return of property sold by the company if he believes that such property was disposed of with the intention of defrauding the company, its members or creditors;[19] and

- exercise their powers in any other EU Member State.[20]

---

[16] S.13(6) of the Companies (Amendment) Act 1990.

[17] S.7 of the Companies (Amendment) Act 1990 as amended by s.18 of the Companies (Amendment) (No. 2) Act 1999

[18] S.297 of the Companies Act 1963 as amended by s.137 of the Companies Act 1990 and s.297A of the Companies Act 1963 as amended by s.138 of the Companies Act 1990.

[19] S.180(2) of the Companies Act 1990.

[20] European Insolvency Regulations, which came into operation on May 31, 2002.

If the examiner fails to get the co-operation of the directors of the company in examination, shadow directors, company officers or connected persons, those persons shall be liable to be prosecuted for criminal offences. If convicted summarily, they shall each be guilty of an offence, which is punishable by a fine of €1,900 and/or one year imprisonment. The fine can be as high as €12,700 and/or five years imprisonment if the are convicted on indictment.

EXAMINER'S REPORT

The primary obligation of the examiner is to report to the court. The court will negotiate an agreement between the shareholders, the company and the creditors if the examiner believes there is a reasonable prospect of survival. Once appointed, the examiner prepares a Scheme of Arrangement, and holds meetings of creditors and members. The proposals contained in the examiner's Scheme of Arrangement are deemed to have been accepted when creditors representing a majority of the claim, support them at a specially convened creditors' meeting. Once he has the required majority backing, he then reports back to the court in order to have the Scheme of Arrangement sanctioned. He has 35 days to do this, but the time period may be extended with the leave of the court.

Court approval of the examiner's report has the effect of binding the affected parties. The court can approve in full or modify the Scheme of Arrangement. The court will sanction the proposals on condition that they:

- have been approved at not less than one class of creditors whose interests would be adversely affected by their implementation;

- are deemed to be fair and equitable as regards groups of creditors or members who have not supported them; and

- do not unfairly prejudice any interested party.[21]

The court at the hearing will consider objections from creditors or members who believe their interests are not properly served by the implementation of the Scheme of Arrangement.

Where important changes are made by the court, members and creditors must meet to consider same. If the court declines to make the changes suggested by members representing a majority of the claim value, the company may be liquidated.

Costs of Examinership

The examiner's remuneration and payment of expenses are treated as matters of priority. In normal circumstances, they are covered by a provision in the Scheme of Arrangement. The costs will not be covered if the examiner breaches his duties. But in the normal course, he is entitled to be paid a salary and expenses, which are deemed reasonable by the court. The examiner can also certify expenses but only those, which have been incurred during the period in which the company has had the protection of the court. However such expenses, while they take priority over other debts, do not have priority over secured creditors.

---

[21] S.24(4) of the Companies (Amendment) Act 1990 as amended by s.180(1)(i) of the Companies Act 1990 and s.24 of the Companies (Amendment) (No. 2) Act 1999.

CHAPTER 9

Receivers

A receiver is appointed by a creditor whose debt has been secured by a charge on some or all of the company's assets. The purpose of a receiver is to take control of an asset, which is the subject of a charge or debenture and deal with it in such a way, which satisfies the debt.[1]

The difference between receivers and receiver managers should be noted. A receiver will be appointed in respect of a specific asset but a receiver manager takes control where the entire business of the company is the subject of the debenture. The receiver manager supervises the company's business for the duration of the receivership.

APPOINTMENT

Usually, the receiver is appointed under a provision of a debenture secured over an asset, which is in danger. The conditions normally include:

- where the debt has not been repaid;

- when the company ceases trading;

- where the principal of the debt is paid but the interest remains owing;

- where there is a petition to wind up the company or where the company passes a resolution for it to be voluntarily wound up; and

- where there is a risk that some of the assets could be seized

---

[1] The principal statutory provisions are included in Pt VII of the Companies Act 1963 and Pt VII of the Companies Act 1990.

or taken to pay monies, which are less important than those of the creditor.

The court may also appoint the receiver. Recourse is normally had to the courts when debenture holders, although they may not have experienced default under the terms of the debenture, fear that their security in the asset in question is at risk. Debenture holders must at all times act in good faith.

In instances where holders of a debenture secured on a floating charge appoint a receiver in relation to all or most of the property of a given company, notice of appointment needs to be given to the company which is then obliged to make a statement of its affairs and swear an affidavit. These documents must be given to the receiver within a fortnight of his appointment. The receiver in turn must send this to the company, the CRO, the debenture holders and their trustees. Where the receiver is appointed by the High Court, these documents are sent to this court – along with a note of any of the receiver's comments.

A receiver cannot be appointed where an examiner is already in place. A receiver may be asked to stop his work if an examiner is appointed within three days of commencing work. As the receiver is the agent of the company, he cannot act where the company is dissolved.

Qualification of a Receiver

There are no specific qualifications required but in the normal course, receivers are practising accountants. Persons precluded from being examiners include:

- corporate bodies, undischarged bankrupts and persons otherwise connected with the company; and

- persons who have been precluded from acting as receivers.

A receiver is either an officer of the **Company** or an officer of the **Court.**

Officer of the Company

When he is appointed under a debenture, he is more likely to be an agent of the company, which is responsible for his acts and remuneration. While he is an agent of the company, he is personally liable for contracts entered into on behalf of the company. His main role is to gets debts repaid and not to manage the company. The company cannot dismiss him.

Officer of the Court

When the court appoints him, he must have regard to the interests of all of the creditors. He is appointed by the court when the debenture document does not give sufficient power to any single creditor to appoint a receiver. The courts will only appoint a receiver:

• where the creditors' secured assets are at risk; or

• where the debenture/charge doesn't otherwise provide for the appointment of a receiver out of court.

Floating charges crystallise. In other words, some of the assets over which there are charges become unsaleable. This prohibits the company from dealing with those assets, which are the subject of a charge.

The legal status of the company does not change. But directors cease to have authority unless legal action is taken in the name of the company and for the benefit of the company. The consent of the receiver is required. Existing contracts are binding but the receiver is not liable.

If existing contracts are adopted by him in his capacity as receiver, he may be liable. Unless any new contracts specifically exclude personal liability, he may be held personally responsible. In the normal course, he is entitled to be reimbursed for any loss suffered as a result of that personal liability. The receiver can sell as much of the company's assets as are covered in the debenture.

Invariably, the debenture will give the receiver the power of attorney and will permit him to perform all duties, which are regarded as necessary to enforce the security of the creditors.

The position of employees is safeguarded by an EU regulation on the Transfer of Undertakings. However, the receiver is not personally liable for the payment of wages.

POWERS OF A RECEIVER

The powers of a receiver are determined by the High Court when he is appointed by this court. Normally, these powers allow the receiver to collect the companies assets and dispose of them in a manner which is consistent with the interests of the court.

In contrast, the powers of the receiver who is appointed on foot of a debenture are determined by the terms of the debenture itself. If he is merely a receiver, he will have the power to take possession of and sell all company property. Whereas if he is a receiver manager, he will have the power to conduct the company's business, to borrow capital, to recruit and lay off staff and to compromise the company's debts.

A receiver may apply to the High Court for an order preventing a director or other company officers from reducing the company's assets below a level set by the court or from removing assets from this jurisdiction.[2] He must demonstrate

---

[2] S.55 of the Company Law Enforcement Act 2001.

that there are good reasons to fear that the assets will be sold or removed with the intention of evading obligations under the Companies Acts.

A receiver can apply to the High Court to have property returned to the company, which was previously removed for the purpose of perpetrating a fraud.[3]

A receiver may bring proceedings against directors, company officers or connected persons who he believes have been engaging in fraudulent or reckless trading.[4]

Guilty parties may be held personally liable if they are found to have been knowingly a party to the carrying on of company business with the intent to defraud creditors for a fraudulent purpose. Furthermore, if the Court forms the view such persons are guilty of fraudulent acts, a fine of €63,000 and/or a jail sentence of up to seven years may be imposed. Parties suspected of reckless trading may be pursued for damages in the civil courts.

The receiver can apply to the High Court if he seeks clarification of his powers.[5] If a receiver is appointed to a company to which a liquidator is subsequently appointed, the former's appointment is not technically affected. But the court may order that the receiver restrict his own work or indeed stop altogether.[6]

DUTIES OF A RECEIVER

Where the receiver is appointed under the terms of a debenture, his status is determined by its terms and he is

---

[3] S.178 of the Companies Act 1990.

[4] S.297 of the Companies Act 1963 as amended by s.137 of the Companies Act 1990 and s.297A of the Companies Act 1963 as amended by s.138 of the Companies Act 1990.

[5] S.316 of the Companies Act 1963 as amended by s.171 of the Companies Act 1990.

[6] S.322B of the Companies Act 1963 as inserted by s.176 of the Companies Act 1990.

generally speaking an agent of the debenture holder. Inasmuch, he has a fiduciary duty. In other words, he is obliged to act in the interests of the debenture holder – even when those interests clash with his own.

Failure to fulfil this duty properly may leave the receiver open to a civil action for damages arising out of his own negligence. Criminal prosecutions may be brought against the receiver where he is suspected of committing a criminal offence under the Companies Acts.

Where he is appointed by the court, he is regarded as an officer of the court and as such, must protect the interests of the company's creditors.

The receiver has a common law duty of care, which flows from his fiduciary duty. So for instance, when he is selling a piece of property, he is obliged to get the best price reasonably available at the time of sale.[7] This duty is owed to the company and to those affected by the actions of the receiver.

A receiver who disregards this obligation is not entitled to be compensated by the company for any debts incurred.

The receiver has a statutory duty of care, which, if disregarded, may leave the receiver personally liable.[8]

The receiver must notify the company's creditors of his plan to dispose of non-cash assets to officers or former officers of the company.[9]

The receiver is under a statutory duty to provide returns to the CRO every six months and at the conclusion of his work.[10] These accounts must include details of payments received and made as well as information regarding the company's assets of which he has taken possession, their value and where the proceeds went.

---

[7] S.316A of the Companies Act 1963 as inserted by s.172 of the Companies Act 1990.

[8] S.316(a) of the Companies Act 1963.

[9] S.316A(3) of the Companies Act 1963 as inserted by s.172 of the Companies Act 1990.

[10] S.319(2) of the Companies Act 1963 as amended by s.52 of the Company Law Enforcement Act 2001.

The receiver, where he ceases to act, must send to the CRO a statement in which he sets out his view on the company's solvency or otherwise.[11]

The receiver has a duty to provide information to the board of the company. The extent of the duty depends on the facts of each case.

The receiver has a duty of care to guarantors of the company's debts. In a situation where there is a shortfall in the amount owed to the debenture holder, a guarantor can sue the receiver for negligence if he feels that the best price was not achieved when certain assets were sold.

The receiver should provide commercial information to the company's directors but there is no general or statutory duty regarding same.

If the receiver is appointed under a fixed charge, he pays the debenture holders and any surplus goes back to the company.

If the receiver is appointed under a floating charge, he pays the preferential shareholders first and then the debenture holders. Only after that does any surplus go back to the company.

The receiver must send a report to the Director of Public Prosecutions if he comes to the belief that over the course of his receivership, a company officer – past or present – has been guilty of a criminal offence under the Companies Acts.

As and from June 1, 2002, the receiver is required to produce for inspection by the Director of Corporate Enforcement all of his books in relation to a specific receivership or any receivership concluded within six years of the date of request. Failure to fulfil this obligation amounts to a criminal offence.[12] He shall be liable to a fine of up to €1,900 and/or a jail term of up to one year if

---

[11] S.319(2A) of the Companies Act 1963 as amended by s.52 of the Company Law Enforcement Act 2001.

[12] S.323A of the Companies Act 1963 as inserted by s.53 Company Law Enforcement Act 2001.

convicted summarily. The penalty can be as high as €12,700 and/or as long as five years imprisonment if he is convicted on indictment.

REMOVAL OF A RECEIVER

The receiver can be removed if:

- the court decides it is in the interest of creditors or if it believes he is guilty of misconduct;

- a liquidator applies to the court to have the receivership limited or terminated;

- the debenture holder removes him under the terms of the debenture; or

- an examiner is appointed within three days of the receiver's appointment.

The receiver can, if appointed by the court, retire but not without the consent of the court. If appointed by a debenture, he must give notice of one month to the holders of floating charges over the whole or part of the company property, the company itself or the holders of fixed charges over the whole or part of the company property.

If the receiver becomes disqualified, failure to resign immediately constitutes a criminal offence. A receiver is regarded as disqualified if he:

- is an undischarged bankrupt;

- has been an officer of the company within the preceding year;

- is a body corporate; or

- is a parent, spouse, partner or sibling of an officer or employee.

CHAPTER 10

Liquidators

Also known as the winding up of a company, liquidation is the process whereby a company's activities cease and it is legally dissolved. Its assets are realised, the creditors are paid off – subject to the company's ability to so do. Any available surplus is distributed to the company's members.

Liquidators, who carry out the winding up of the company, do not need specific qualifications but in the normal course, are professional accountants.[1] That said, a fitness to practice certificate must be produced to the court in the event of a compulsory liquidation.[2] Furthermore, undischarged bankrupts, persons associated with officers or employees of the liquidated company or persons otherwise disqualified, may not act as Liquidators.

DUTIES OF A LIQUIDATOR

A liquidator must:

- act responsibly as an officer of the Court;

- inquire into the company's business;

- take possession of its property, assets and all documents related to its business;

- make a list of the company's creditors and contributories, those who must contribute to the assets of the company when it is being wound up;

---

[1] For more on the legislative provisions, see ss. 225–231 of the of the Companies Act 1963, ss. 129–145 of the of the Companies Act 1990 and ss. 43–58 of the Company Law Enforcement Act 2001.

[2] See below at p.112.

- have disputed cases determined by the court;

- call a final general meeting of the company – in the case of a creditors' voluntary liquidation – to explain how he has conducted the winding up;[3]

- call a creditors' meeting – in the case of a members' voluntary liquidation – if he thinks the company will have difficulties paying its debts;[4]

- discharge its debts;

- distribute any surplus among members in proportion to their entitlements;

- call a general meeting or in the case of a creditors' liquidation, a creditors' meeting each year if the winding up is not complete, to give an account of his work; and

- in the case of a court-appointed liquidator, to report to the High Court Examiner in relation to the performance of his duties and to apply to court for directions regarding any remaining monies.

NEW OBLIGATIONS ON THE LIQUIDATOR FOLLOWING THE ENACTMENT OF THE COMPANY LAW ENFORCEMENT ACT 2001

As and from June 1, 2002, the liquidator of an insolvent company is required to send a report to the Director of Corporate Enforcement on the conduct of the directors.[5] This reporting provision applies to all liquidators appointed to insolvent companies on or after June 1, 2002 or to liquidators appointed on or after July 1, 2001 where the liquidation was continuing on June 1, 2002. The report must set out the liquidator's views on how the directors have conducted

---

[3] S.263 of the Companies Act 1963.

[4] S.261 of the Companies Act 1963 as amended by s.129 of the Companies Act 1990.

[5] S.56(1) of the Company Law Enforcement Act 2001.

themselves, whether they should be restricted or disqualified where there was evidence of an offence under the Companies Acts.

Liquidators must also apply to the High Court for an order restricting all of the company's directors unless expressly relieved by the Director of Corporate Enforcement.[6]

If the liquidator fails to file this report or does not apply for an order restricting all of the company's directors in instances where he has not be so relieved by the Director of Corporate Enforcement, he shall be guilty of an offence which is punishable by a fine of €1,900 and/ or one year imprisonment if tried summarily.[7] The fine can be as high as €12,700 and/or five years imprisonment if he is convicted on indictment.

In the normal course of events, the liquidator must bear the costs of this application but under the 2001 Act, the court can make an order for costs against the restricted directors.[8]

When a voluntary liquidator believes that a company officer or member has committed a criminal offence – past or present – he must report the matter to the Director of Corporate Enforcement and to the Director of Public Prosecutions. In so doing, the liquidator must provide the Director of Corporate Enforcement with all information and documents, which relate to the criminal offence.[9]

In the case of an official liquidation, the court can order the liquidator to provide a report to the Director of Corporate Enforcement and to the Director of Public Prosecutions where he feels that a criminal offence may have been committed by a company officer or member – past or present. The liquidator

---

[6] S.56(2) of the Company Law Enforcement Act 2001. For more on this, see Chap.5 on *Directors: Appointment, Remuneration and Removal*.

[7] S.56(3) of the Company Law Enforcement Act 2001.

[8] S.150(4B) of the Companies Act 1990 as inserted by s.41 of the Company Law Enforcement Act 2001.

[9] S.299(2A) of the Companies Act 1963 as inserted by s.51 of the Company Law Enforcement Act 2001.

is obliged to facilitate the Director of Corporate Enforcement in getting access to relevant documents.[10]

As and from June 1, 2002, the liquidator must provide the Director of Corporate Enforcement with access to all his books, which relate not just to a particular liquidation process but also to all liquidations completed by him in the preceding six years. He must also make himself available for questioning in relation to the books supplied.[11] Liquidators must file certain returns to the CRO.

If the liquidator is in breach of any of the above duties, he shall be guilty of an offence, which is punishable by a fine of €1,900 and/or one year imprisonment if tried summarily. The fine can be as high as €12,700 and/or five years imprisonment if he is convicted on indictment.

Types of Liquidation

There are three types of liquidation:

- Compulsory/Official Liquidation.

- Voluntary Liquidation.

- Striking Off The Company Register.

Compulsory/Official Liquidator

This is where the court appoints the liquidator. The members of the company have no input provided it is on foot of a creditors' petition. The court will appoint a liquidator if it thinks it is just and equitable. Among the persons who can petition to have the company wound-up are

- the company;

- the creditors;

---

[10] S.299(1A) of the Companies Act 1963 as inserted by s.51 of the Company Law Enforcement Act 2001.

[11] S.57 of the Company Law Enforcement Act 2001.

- the members;

- the contributories, defined as those who are liable to contribute to the assets of the company in the event of it being wound up;

- the Minister for Enterprise, Trade and Employment;

- the CRO; or

- the Director of Corporate Enforcement.

Grounds for the appointment of an official liquidator

Inability to pay debts.[12] This is covered in the 1963 Act and covers situations where a creditors' 21-day letter demanding repayment of a debt of at least €1,269 is not satisfied or where the sheriff unsuccessfully tries to execute a decree, judgment or court order. Where it is "just and equitable" that the com-pany be wound up.

Where the company is solvent, but its Articles of Association stipulate that it be wound up after a particular period of time or if the members or shareholders pass a resolution that the company be liquidated in order to distribute its assets. A copy of the resolution must be submitted along with a declaration of solvency sworn by a majority of the directors and a report from an independent person stating that the declaration of solvency is and statement of affairs are accurate. This is in order to protect creditors' interests.

Where the court believes that the company is being managed in a way, which is oppressive to any member or is in disregard of their interests. The court needs to be convinced that some other remedy under section 205 of the 1963 Act – such as a buy-out of shares – would not give an adequate remedy.

The official liquidator is appointed after the court is presented with a petition by the creditors who must satisfy

---

[12] S.213(e) of the Companies Act 1963.

the court that there is no dispute as to the debt outstanding. The company can contest that there are no *bona fide* grounds to the petitioners' claim or indeed it can compromise the claim by paying off the debt and having the petition struck out.

If the court decides in favour of the petitioner, an order winding up the company is made and the official liquidator, usually the nominee of the petitioner, is duly appointed. He has similar powers to those of a voluntary liquidator[13] but he is subject to the control of the court, which fixes the payment and other conditions.

Implications of the appointment of an official liquidator

The order winding up the company takes effect from the date of the presentation of the petition. The company must cease trading immediately unless it is beneficial for the liquidation for it to continue to trade.

The company's position in relation to its own assets is similar to that of a trustee.

Court approval is required if any proceedings are to be taken against the company.

Unless otherwise stated in the Articles of Association, the company's separate legal personality as well as its powers continue until the company is dissolved.[14] As soon as a voluntary liquidator is appointed, it is assumed that the company's powers transfer to the liquidator. The directors' powers pass to the liquidator. Any invoices sent out by the company must state clearly that it is in the process of liquidation.

Unless the liquidator engages in fraud, personal misconduct or bad faith, he will not be liable for losses incurred by the company.

The liquidator is entitled to information from the directors who are obliged to complete a statement of affairs. The

---

[13] See below, p.115.
[14] S.254 of the Companies Act 1963.

liquidator can disown property to which onerous obligations attach.

Any party will be in contempt of court if he fails to attend a meeting with a liquidator who has received a court order.

The liquidator can apply to the court for a *Mareva* injunction if he feels that the company's assets may be removed from the jurisdiction or otherwise disposed of. The liquidator may not dispose of property held in trust.

Floating charges become invalid if they are created within 12 months of the appointment of a liquidator. An exception is made if the company was solvent after the charge was created.

Voluntary Liquidator

The liquidator is chosen by the members or the creditors. The courts are not involved. It is an inexpensive and convenient way of liquidating a company. A members' winding-up may be converted into a creditors' winding-up in any of three ways:

- if creditors representing not less than 20% of the value of the company apply to the court within 28 days of the members advertising for voluntary liquidation;

- if the members' liquidator is of the view that the company will not be able to pay its debts within a period of time set out in the solvency declaration, he can call a meeting at which he can be replaced by a creditors' liquidator; or

- if the members' liquidator applies to court within seven days of finding out that there is no report from an independent person accompanying the declaration of solvency, the liquidation is taken over by the creditors.

The directors of a company may wind up their company if they believe that the company is insolvent. They are obliged to place a statement of the company's affairs before separate meetings of the members and of the creditors. At the members' EGM, of which seven days notice must be given, a resolution is passed declaring that the company cannot continue trading because of its debts and that it should be voluntarily liquidated.

The creditors appoint a liquidator by reference to a majority of their value only – and not by number and value as was previously the case.[15]

The company must stop trading immediately and the members' liquidator then commences his task. He can be replaced by a creditors' liquidator at their meeting, which must be held on the same day or the day after the members' meeting.

Notice of the creditors' meeting must be given in the daily papers circulating in the area of the company's registered office. This meeting is given a statement of affairs, is allowed retain or replace the member's liquidator and may appoint a committee of inspection comprising not more than five creditors to supervise the liquidation process. Only creditors who have unchallenged debts can vote.

Members, creditors or a combination of both can apply to convert a voluntary liquidation into a compulsory liquidation on application to the court. If the court is of the opinion that the voluntarily appointed liquidator has refused to put in place a declaration of solvency or refuses to investigate directors' misdeeds, then the court can convert the winding-up into a compulsory one. In so doing, the court will consider the views of creditors but there must be compelling reasons to convert the liquidation.

Duties of a voluntary liquidator

A liquidator's function is to realise and distribute the company's assets in accordance with the Companies Acts. He is the agent of the company and takes over its management role.

---

[15] S.47 of the Company Law Enforcement Act inserted by s.267(3) of the Companies Act 1963.

A liquidator must honour pre-existing deals with creditors, if supported by a special resolution of members or by three-quarters of creditors.

A liquidator must, if appointed by creditors, convene a creditors' meeting at the end of the first year of the winding-up process and at the end of each subsequent year.

A liquidator must, if appointed by members, convene a meeting of creditors where, despite the declaration of solvency, he believes that company is insolvent.

A liquidator must get the authority of the committee of inspection, the creditors or the court if he can pay in full a class of creditors or to make any repayment arrangement with them.

A liquidator must get the authority of the committee of inspection or of the court if he is to compromise or make any arrangement with contributories. The liquidator must await the outcome of a meeting of creditors before he can exercise power;

The liquidator may not sell non-cash assets to any individual who was an officer of the company within three years before the winding-up unless there is 14 days notice to creditors.

With the permission of the court, a written disclaimer can be signed by the liquidator regarding property, which is unsaleable due to onerous duties that may attach.

The liquidator must give an account of the liquidation to a general meeting held within 28 days of notices being posted in two newspapers circulated in the area in which the company's registered office is located. This account needs to be sent to the Companies Registration Office within seven days of the meeting. The company is considered dissolved 90 days afterwards.

A liquidator appointed by the court needs the leave of the court to:

• initiate or defend any legal action on behalf of the company including the appointment of a legal adviser;

- conduct business on behalf of the company in order to secure its successful liquidation;

- discharge debts to or compromise arrangements with creditors; or

- compromise all calls and liabilities to calls of contributories.

A provisional liquidator's function is to preserve the company's assets so that they can be realised and distributed after the High Court makes the order to liquidate the company. The High Court takes away the powers of the directors and may allow the provisional liquidator to carry on the business of the company if it is beneficial to the liquidation process.

Powers of a voluntary liquidator

A liquidator has unfettered powers to

- initiate or defend any legal or other action in the name of or on behalf of the company;

- carry on trading for as long as is necessary;

- dispose of the company's cash reserves, chattels or real estate;

- execute all deeds in the name of the company;

- take out loans and give corporate assets as security;

- appoint assistants or agents; and

- do whatever is necessary for the successful winding-up and distribution of the assets among creditors.

The liquidator appointed by members is allowed to accept shares in a contributory company in consideration for the sale of the property in the company, which is being wound up. Members must give their consent by way of a special resolution. The approval of the committee of inspection is required for a similar action to be carried out by a liquidator appointed by creditors.

The liquidator – whether appointed officially or voluntarily – may apply to the court for directions.

The liquidator may convene a general meeting of the company if he believes there is good reason.[16] The liquidator, in order to facilitate the winding up of the company, can disclaim any of the company's property if he deems it to be more of a liability than an asset.[17]

The liquidator may seek the permission of the High Court for an order directing that a profitable parent company or subsidiary company contribute some of its assets to a related company being wound up. Where two related companies are being wound up, the liquidator can apply for an order directing that the assets of both companies be pooled.[18]

The liquidator can apply for an order to void a transaction entered into by an insolvent company if it constituted a fraudulent preference. An application of this kind can be made within two years of the transaction being made in favour of a person connected with the company. A transaction is assumed to have been made with the intention of favouring a connected person unless the contrary can be shown. However, in the normal event, the liquidator must prove it was the intention to favour the creditor in question.[19]

The liquidator can apply to the court for an order for the return of property sold by the insolvent company, if he has reason to believe that it was disposed of in order to perpetrate fraud.[20]

The liquidator can bring proceedings against company officers, shadow directors or connected persons for fraudulent or reckless trading. If found guilty, they can be held personally

---

[16] S.276 of the Companies Act 1963 as amended by s.131 of the Companies Act 1990.

[17] S.290 of the Companies Act 1963.

[18] S.141 of the Companies Act 1990.

[19] S.286 of the Companies Act 1963 as amended by s.135 of the Companies Act 1990.

[20] S.139 of the Companies Act 1990.

liable and may have penal sanctions imposed including imprisonment.[21] Similar sanctions can be imposed on persons who are found to have been a party to the carrying on of business with the intention to defraud creditors. Before making any such finding, the court will try to satisfy itself that such persons acted honestly and reasonably in relation to their dealings with the company.

The liquidator can bring proceedings for the recovery of property or money which in his opinion has been misapplied or wrongfully retained by directors or connected persons in a company which is insolvent.

The liquidator can apply to the High Court for an order imposing personal liability on company directors who have not maintained proper books of account.[22]

LIQUIDATOR'S NEW POWERS FOLLOWING THE ENACTMENT OF THE COMPANY LAW ENFORCEMENT ACT 2001

Several more powers have been given to Liquidators in order to assist them in their investigation of the company and the realisation of its assets. They are:

• The power to apply to the High Court for an order summoning a company officer or relevant person for examination.[23] This is a power, which is shared with the Director of Corporate Enforcement.

Where this happens, the court can compel the attendance of any person who it believes can give useful information

---

[21] S.297 of the Companies Act 1963 as amended by s.137 of the Companies Act 1990 and s.297A of the Companies Act 1963 as amended by s.138 of the Companies Act 1990.

[22] S.204 of the Companies Act 1990.

[23] S.245 of the Companies Act 1963 as amended by s.282B of the Companies Act 1963, s.126 of the Companies Act 1990 and s.44 of the Company Law Enforcement Act 2001.

about the company. This can include company officers who may have company property, money or documents. Failure to attend constitutes contempt of court and can be punished by terms of imprisonment or financial penalties. The court can order persons summonsed to appear before it to repay money or hand over property or documents.

Information collated from such an inspection may be shared with the CRO, An Garda Síochána, the Criminal Assets Bureau, the Minister for Enterprise, Trade and Employment, her officials and agents. It may also be passed on to counterpart authorities in other states – within the European Union and without.

• The power to make a civil arrest.[24]

The liquidator can apply to the High Court for an order to arrest a contributory to the company so as to stop such a person from removing the property, avoiding the payment of money owed or leaving the jurisdiction. He can also apply for an order freezing the company's assets where it is believed that a company officer is likely to disperse the assets or take them out of the jurisdiction.

• The right to exercise his powers in other EU Member States.[25]

Striking off the Company Register

If a company is in breach of the Companies Acts, it can be struck off. This can happen where the company has ceased

---

[24] S.245(8) of the Companies Act 1963 as amended by s.126 of the Companies Act 1990 and s.44 of the Company Law Enforcement Act 2001.

[25] European Insolvency Regulations, which came into force on May 31, 2002.

trading or where it has failed to submit returns for two consecutive years.[26]

If the company fails to file returns for any single year, the CRO can send a letter to the company warning that it will be struck off within one month unless it cooperates. If struck off, ownership of the company's property passes to the State. Notwithstanding this, the liability of the officers, members and directors will not be affected. The company must be reinstated by the court if it wishes to appoint an official liquidator.

The company can be restored to the companies register if the company, any creditor or member applies to the court within 20 years of being struck off. The company can seek to be reinstated only if it feels it has been unfairly treated and it fulfils its obligations in relation to returns. The court will reinstate the company if it can be proved that the company was trading when it was struck off and that it is just and equitable for it to be restored.

As a matter of right, a creditor is entitled to an order winding up a company if that company cannot pay its debts. The court may refuse the application if it feels that it is an abuse of process or that a majority of creditors are opposed to the appointment of a liquidator.

DISTRIBUTION OF ASSETS[27]

The liquidator's costs and expenses take priority over the claims of creditors unless the creditor has a fixed charge over an asset. He can make interim distribution orders to pay his costs and expenses.

Secured creditors do not have to bring claims in the liquidation process and can rely on their security to have their debts repaid. In a compulsory liquidation, the court can make

---

[26] S.245 of the Companies Act 1990.

[27] S.285 of the Companies Act 1963 as amended by s.10 of the Companies (Amendment) Act 1982.

an order prioritising the payment of costs where the value of the assets is less than the amount of the debts. The following list of priorities is used by the liquidator when distributing assets:

- secured creditors;

- liquidator's remuneration and expenses;

- the Revenue Commissioners and employees;

- holders of floating charges;

- unsecured creditors; and

- contributories and members.

Glossary of Terms

Affidavit: A sworn written statement

AGM: Annual General Meeting. Every company must hold one such meeting each year.

Articles of Association: The rules by which a company agrees to operate.

Bankrupt: Someone who has is financially unable to comply with an order of a court to pay a creditor.

EGM: A meeting other than an AGM.

***Ex-parte*:** Without notice to the other party in legal proceedings.

Fiduciary: Someone to whom powers have been given in trust.

Immunity: Exemption from liability.

Indictable offence: A serious offence triable before a judge and jury.

Injunction: A court order directing that someone to do or refrain from doing something specific.

Limited liability: Personal indemnity enjoyed by members of a company in the event of the business not being successful.

Memorandum of Association: The fundamental law of a company.

Ordinary resolution: A vote which requires a simple majority (51%) of the votes cast by eligible members.

Pre-emption rights: The rights to purchase shares or property before anyone else.

***Prima facie*:** On initial examination.

Proxy: Someone who is delegated to vote in a certain way on behalf of another person.

Quorum: The minimum number of persons needed for a

meeting to validly take place.

Special resolution: A vote which requires the support of 75% of the votes cast by eligible members.

Stamp duty: Taxes raised by the requirement to have certain legal documents stamped by regulatory authorities.

Sub judice: Under consideration of a court.

Subpoena: An order directing a person to attend a specific court at a specific date on fear of penal sanction.

Summary offence: A less serious offence, which can be tried by a judge alone.

Ultra Vires: Outside the power designated to a person or company.

Articles of Association

TABLE A

PART I

REGULATIONS FOR MANAGEMENT OF A COMPANY LIMITED BY SHARES NOT BEING A PRIVATE COMPANY

Interpretation

1. —In these regulations:

"the Act" means the Companies Act, 1963 (No. 33 of 1963);

"the directors" means the directors for the time being of the company or the directors present at a meeting of the board of directors and includes any person occupying the position of director by whatever name called;

"the register" means the register of members to be kept as required by section 116 of the Act;

"secretary" means any person appointed to perform the duties of the secretary of the company;

"the office" means the registered office for the time being of the company;

"the seal" means the common seal of the company.

Expressions referring to writing shall, unless the contrary intention appears, be construed as including references to printing, lithography, photography, and any other modes of representing or reproducing words in a visible form.

Unless the contrary intention appears, words or expressions contained in these regulations shall bear the same meaning as in the Act or in any statutory modification thereof in force at the date at which these regulations become binding on the company.

Share Capital and Variation of Rights

2.—Without prejudice to any special rights previously conferred on the holders of any existing shares or class of shares, any share in the company may be issued with such preferred, deferred or other special rights or such restrictions, whether in regard to dividend, voting, return of capital or otherwise, as the company may from time to time by ordinary "resolution determine.

3.—If at any time the share capital is divided into different classes of shares, the rights attached to any class (unless otherwise provided by the terms of issue of the shares of that class) may, whether or not the company is being wound up, be varied or abrogated with the consent in writing of the holders of three-fourths of the issued shares of that class, or with the sanction of a special resolution passed at a separate general meeting of the holders of the shares of the class. To every such separate general meeting the provisions of these regulations relating to general meetings shall apply but so that the necessary quorum shall be two persons at least holding or representing by proxy one-third of the issued shares of the class. If at any adjourned meeting of such holders a quorum as above defined is not present those members who are present shall be a quorum. Any holders of shares of the class present in person or by proxy may demand a poll.

4.—The rights conferred upon the holders of the shares of any class issued with preferred or other rights shall not, unless otherwise expressly provided by the terms of issue of the shares of that class, be deemed to be varied by the creation or issue of further shares ranking *pari passu* therewith.

5.—Subject to the provisions of these regulations relating to new shares, the shares shall be at the disposal of the directors, and they may (subject to the provisions of the Act) allot, grant options over or otherwise dispose of them to such persons, on such terms and conditions and at such times as they may consider to be in the best interests of the company and its shareholders, but so that no share shall be issued at a discount, except in accordance with the provisions of the Act, and so that in the case of shares offered to the public for subscription, the amount payable on application on each share shall not be less than 5 per cent of the nominal amount of the share.

6.—The company may exercise the powers of paying commissions conferred by section 59 of the Act, provided that the rate per cent and the amount of the commission paid or agreed to be paid shall be disclosed in the manner required by that section, and the rate of the commission shall not exceed the rate of 10 per cent of the price at which the shares in respect whereof the same is paid are issued or an amount equal to 10 per cent of such price (as the case may be). Such commission may be satisfied by the payment of cash or the allotment of fully or partly paid shares or partly in one way and partly in the other. The company may also, on any issue of shares, pay such brokerage as may be lawful.

7.—Except as required by law, no person shall be recognised by the company as holding any share upon any trust, and the company shall not be bound by or be compelled in any way to recognise (even when having notice thereof) any equitable, contingent, future or partial interest in any share or any interest in any fractional part of a share or (except only as by these regulations or by law otherwise provided) any other rights in respect of any share except an absolute right to the entirety thereof in the registered holder: this shall not preclude the company from requiring the members or a transferee of shares to furnish the company with information as to the beneficial ownership of any share when such information is reasonably required by the company.

8.—Every person whose name is entered as a member in the register shall be entitled without payment to receive within

2 months after allotment or lodgment of a transfer (or within such other period as the conditions of issue shall provide) one certificate for all his shares or several certificates each for one or more of his shares upon payment of 2s. 6d. for every certificate after the first or such less sum as the directors shall from time to time determine, so, however, that in respect of a share or shares held jointly by several persons the company shall not be bound to issue more than one certificate, and delivery of a certificate for a share to one of several joint holders shall be sufficient delivery to all such holders. Every certificate shall be under the seal and shall specify the shares to which it relates and the amount paid up thereon.

9.—If a share certificate be defaced, lost or destroyed, it may be renewed on payment of 2s. 6d. or such less sum and on such terms (if any) as to evidence and indemnity and the payment of out-of-pocket expenses of the company of investigating evidence as the directors think fit.

10.—The company shall not give, whether directly or indirectly, and whether by means of a loan, guarantee, the provision of security or otherwise, any financial assistance for the purpose of or in connection with a purchase or subscription made or to be made by any person of or for any shares in the company or in its holding company, but this regulation shall not prohibit any transaction permitted by section 60 of the Act.

Lien

11.—The company shall have a first and paramount lien on every share (not being a fully paid share) for an moneys (whether immediately payable or not) called or payable at a fixed time in respect of that share, and the company shall also have a first and paramount lien on all shares (other than fully paid shares) standing registered in the name of a single person for all moneys immediately payable by him or his estate to the company; but the directors may at any time declare any share to be wholly or in part exempt from the provisions of this regulation. The company's lien on a share shall extend to all dividends payable thereon.

12.—The company may sell, in such manner as the directors think fit, any shares on which the company has a lien, but no sale shall be made unless a sum in respect of which the lien exists is immediately payable, nor until the expiration of 14 days after a notice in writing, stating and demanding payment of such part of the amount in respect of which the lien exists as is immediately payable, has been given to the registered holder for the time being of the share, or the person entitled thereto by reason of his death or bankruptcy.

13.—To give effect to any such sale, the directors may authorise some person to transfer the shares sold to the purchaser thereof. The purchaser shall be registered as the holder of the shares comprised in any such transfer, and he shall not be bound to see to the application of the purchase money, nor shall his title to the shares be affected by any irregularity or invalidity in the proceedings in reference to the sale.

14.—The proceeds of the sale shall be received by the company and applied in payment of such part of the amount in respect of which the lien exists as is immediately payable, and the residue, if any, shall (subject to a like lien for sums not immediately payable as existed upon the shares before the sale) be paid to the person entitled to the shares at the date of the sale.

Calls on Shares
15.—The directors may from time to time make calls upon the members in respect of any moneys unpaid on their shares (whether on account of the nominal value of the shares or by way of premium) and not by the conditions of allotment thereof made payable at fixed times, provided that no call

shall exceed one-fourth of the nominal value of the share or be payable at less than one month from the date fixed for the payment of the last preceding call, and each member shall (subject to receiving at least 14 days' notice specifying the time or times and place of payment) pay to the company at the time or times and place so specified the amount called on his shares. A call may be revoked or postponed as the directors may determine.

16.—A call shall be deemed to have been made at the time when the resolution of the directors authorising the call was passed and may be required to be paid by instalments.

17.—The joint holders of a share shall be jointly and severally liable to pay all calls in respect thereof.

18.—If a sum called in respect of a share is not paid before or on the day appointed for payment thereof, the person from whom the sum is due shall pay interest on the sum from the day appointed for payment thereof to the time of actual payment at such rate, not exceeding 5 per cent *per annum*, as the directors may determine, but the directors shall be at liberty to waive payment of such interest wholly or in part.

19.—Any sum which by the terms of issue of a share becomes payable on allotment or at any fixed date, whether on account of the nominal value of the share or by way of premium, shall, for the purposes of these regulations, be deemed to be a call duly made and payable on the date on which, by the terms of issue, the same becomes payable, and in case of non-payment all the relevant provisions of these regulations as to payment of interest and expenses, forfeiture or otherwise, shall apply as if such sum had become payable by virtue of a call duly made and notified.

20.—The directors may, on the issue of shares, differentiate between the holders as to the amount of calls to be paid and the times of payment.

21.—The directors may, if they think fit, receive from any member willing to advance the same, all or any part of the moneys uncalled and unpaid upon any shares held by him, and upon all or any of the moneys so advanced may (until the same would, but for such advance, become payable) pay interest at such rate not exceeding (unless the company in general meeting otherwise directs) 5 per cent *per annum*, as may be agreed upon between the directors and the member paying such sum in advance.

Transfer of Shares

22.—The instrument of transfer of any share shall be executed by or on behalf of the transferor and transferee, and the transferor shall be deemed to remain the holder of the share until the name of the transferee is entered in the register in respect thereof.

23.—Subject to such of the restrictions of these regulations as may be applicable, any member may transfer all or any of his shares by instrument in writing in any usual or common form or any other form which the directors may approve.

24.—The directors may decline to register the transfer of a share (not being a fully paid share) to a person of whom they do not approve, and they may also decline to register the transfer of a share on which the company has a lien. The directors may also decline to register any transfer of a share which, in their opinion, may imperil or prejudicially affect the status of the company in the State or which may imperil any tax concession or rebate to which the members of the company are entitled or which may involve the company in the payment of any additional stamp or other duties on any conveyance of any property made or to be made to the company.

25.—The directors may also decline to recognise any

instrument of transfer unless—

    (*a*) a fee of 2s. 6d. or such lesser sum as the directors may from time to time require, is paid to the company in respect thereof; and

    (*b*) the instrument of transfer is accompanied by the certificate of the shares to which it relates, and such other evidence as the directors may reasonably require to show the right of the transferor to make the transfer; and

    (*c*) the instrument of transfer is in respect of one class of share only.

26.—If the directors refuse to register a transfer they shall, within 2 months after the date on which the transfer was lodged with the company, send to the transferee notice of the refusal.

27.—The registration of transfers may be suspended at such times and for such periods, not exceeding in the whole 30 days in each year, as the directors may from time to time determine.

28.—The company shall be entitled to charge a fee not exceeding 2s. 6d. on the registration of every probate, letters of administration, certificate of death or marriage, power of attorney, notice as to stock or other instrument.

Transmission of Shares

29.—In the case of the death of a member, the survivor or survivors where the deceased was a joint holder, and the personal representatives of the deceased where he was a sole holder, shall be the only persons recognised by the company as having any title to his interest in the shares; but nothing herein contained shall release the estate of a deceased joint holder from any liability in respect of any share which had been jointly held by him with other persons.

30.—Any person becoming entitled to a share in consequence of the death or bankruptcy of a member may, upon such evidence being produced as may from time to time properly be required by the directors and subject as hereinafter provided, elect either to be registered himself as holder of the share or to have some person nominated by him registered as the transferee thereof, but the directors shall, in either case, have the same right to decline or suspend registration as they would have had in the case of a transfer of the share by that member before his death or bankruptcy, as the case may be.

31.—If the person so becoming entitled elects to be registered himself, he shall deliver or send to the company a notice in writing signed by him stating that he so elects. If he elects to have another person registered, he shall testify his election by executing to that person a transfer of the share. All the limitations, restrictions and provisions of these regulations relating to the right to transfer and the registration of transfers of shares shall be applicable to any such notice or transfer as aforesaid as if the death or bankruptcy of the member had not occurred and the notice or transfer were a transfer signed by that member.

32.—A person becoming entitled to a share by reason of the death or bankruptcy of the holder shall be entitled to the same dividends and other advantages to which he would be entitled if he were the registered holder of the share, except that he shall not, before being registered as a member in respect of the share, be entitled in respect of it to exercise any right conferred by membership in relation to meetings of the company, so, however, that the directors may at any time give notice requiring any such person to elect either to be registered himself or to transfer the share, and if the notice is not complied with within 90 days, the directors may thereupon withhold payment of all dividends, bonuses or other moneys payable in respect of the share until the requirements of the notice have been complied with.

Forfeiture of Shares

33.—If a member fails to pay any call or instalment of a call on the day appointed for payment thereof, the directors may, at any time thereafter during such time as any part of the call or instalment remains unpaid, serve a notice on him requiring payment of so much of the call or instalment as is unpaid together with any interest which may have accrued.

34.—The notice shall name a further day (not earlier than the expiration of 14 days from the date of service of the notice) on or before which the payment required by the notice is to be made, and shall state that in the event of non-payment at or before the time appointed the shares in respect of which the call was made will be liable to be forfeited.

35.—If the requirements of any such notice as aforesaid are not complied with, any share in respect of which the notice has been given may at any time thereafter, before the payment required by the notice has been made, be forfeited by a resolution of the directors to that effect.

36.—A forfeited share may be sold or otherwise disposed of on such terms and in such manner as the directors think fit, and at any time before a sale or disposition the forfeiture may be cancelled on such terms as the directors think fit.

37.—A person whose shares have been forfeited shall cease to be a member in respect of the forfeited shares, but shall, notwithstanding, remain liable to pay to the company all moneys which, at the date of forfeiture, were payable by him to the company in respect of the shares, but his liability shall cease if and when the company shall have received payment in full of all such moneys in respect of the shares.

38.—A statutory declaration that the declaration is a director or the secretary of the company, and that a share in the company has been duly forfeited on a date stated in the declaration, shall be conclusive evidence of the facts therein stated as against all persons claiming to be entitled to the share. The company may receive the consideration, if any, given for the share on any sale or disposition thereof and may execute a transfer of the share in favour of the person to whom the share is sold or disposed of and he shall thereupon be registered as the holder of the share, and shall not be bound to see to the application of the purchase money, if any, nor shall his title to the share be affected by any irregularity or invalidity in the proceedings in reference to the forfeiture, sale or disposal of the share.

39.—The provisions of these regulations as to forfeiture shall apply in the case of non-payment of any sum which, by the terms of issue of a share, becomes payable at a fixed time, whether on account of the nominal value of the share or by way of premium, as if the same had been payable by virtue of a call duly made and notified.

Conversion of Shares into Stock

40.—The company may by ordinary resolution convert any paid up shares into stock, and reconvert any stock into paid up shares of any denomination.

41.—The holders of stock may transfer the same, or any part thereof, in the same manner, and subject to the same regulations, as and subject to which the shares from which the stock arose might previously to conversion have been transferred, or as near thereto as circumstances admit; and the directors may from time to time fix the minimum amount of stock transferable but so that such minimum shall not exceed the nominal amount of each share from which the stock arose.

42.—The holders of stock shall, according to the amount of stock held by them, have the same rights, privileges and advantages in relation to dividends, voting at meetings of the company and other matters as if they held the shares from which the stock arose, but no such right, privilege or advantage (except participation in the dividends and profits of the company and in the assets on winding up) shall be conferred by an amount of stock which would not, if existing in shares, have conferred that right privilege or advantage.

43.—Such of the regulations of the company as are applicable to paid up shares shall apply to stock, and the words "share" and "shareholder" therein shall include "stock" and " stockholder".

Alteration of Capital

44.—The company may from time to time by ordinary resolution increase the share capital by such sum, to be divided into shares of such amount, as the resolution shall prescribe.

45.—The company may by ordinary resolution-
- (*a*) consolidate and divide all or any of its share capital into shares of larger amount than its existing shares;
- (*b*) subdivide its existing shares, or any of them, into shares of smaller amount than is fixed by the memorandum of association subject, nevertheless, to section 68(1)(*d*) of the Act;
- (*c*) cancel any shares which, at the date of the passing of the resolution, have not been taken or agreed to be taken by any person.

46.—The company may by special resolution reduce its share capital, any capital redemption reserve fund or any share premium account in any manner and with and subject to any incident authorised, and consent required, by law.

General Meetings

47.—All general meetings of the company shall be held in the State.

48.—(1) Subject to paragraph (2) of this regulation, the company shall in each year hold a general meeting as its annual general meeting in addition to any other meeting in that year, and shall specify the meeting as such in the notices calling it; and not more than 15 months shall elapse between the date of one annual general meeting of the company and that of the next.

(2) So long as the company holds its first annual general meeting within 18 months of its incorporation, it need not hold it in the year of its incorporation or in the year following. Subject to regulation 47, the annual general meeting shall be held at such time and place as the directors shall appoint.

49.—All general meetings other than annual general meetings shall be called extraordinary general meetings.

50.—The directors may, whenever they think fit, convene an extraordinary general meeting, and extraordinary general meetings shall also be convened on such requisition, or in default, may be convened by such requisitionists, as provided by section 132 of the Act. If at any time there are not within the State sufficient directors capable of acting to form a quorum, any director or any 2 members of the company may convene an extraordinary general meeting in the same manner as nearly as possible as that in which meetings may be convened by the directors.

Notice of General Meetings

51.—Subject to sections 133 and 141 of the Act, an annual general meeting and a meeting called for the passing of a special resolution shall be called by 21 days' notice in writing at the least, and a meeting of the company (other than an annual general meeting or a meeting for the passing of a special resolution) shall be called by 14 days' notice in writing at the least. The notice shall be exclusive of the day on which it is served or deemed to be served and of the day for which it is given, and shall specify the place, the day and the hour of the meeting, and in the case of special business, the general nature of that business, and shall be given, in manner hereinafter mentioned, to such persons as are, under the regulations of the company, entitled to receive such notices from the company.

52.—The accidental omission to give notice of a meeting to, or the non-receipt of notice of a meeting by, any person entitled to receive notice shall not invalidate the proceedings at the meeting.

Proceedings at General Meetings

53.—All business shall be deemed special that is transacted at an extraordinary general meeting, and also all that is transacted at an annual general meeting, with the exception of declaring a dividend, the consideration of the accounts, balance sheets and the reports of the directors and auditors, the election of directors in the place of those retiring, the re-appointment of the retiring auditors and the fixing of the remuneration of the auditors.

54.—No business shall be transacted at any general meeting unless a quorum of members is present at the time when the meeting proceeds to business; save as herein otherwise provided, three members present in person shall be a quorum.

55.—If within half an hour from the time appointed for the meeting a quorum is not present, the meeting, if convened upon the requisition of members, shall be dissolved; in any other case it shall stand adjourned to the same day in the next week, at the same time and place or to such other day and at such other time and place as the directors may determine, and if at the adjourned meeting a quorum is not present within half an hour from the time appointed for the meeting, the members present shall be a quorum.

56.—The chairman, if any, of the board of directors shall preside as chairman at every general meeting of the company, or if there is no such chairman, or if he is not present within 15 minutes after the time appointed for the holding of the meeting or is unwilling to act, the directors present shall elect one of their number to be chairman of the meeting.

57.—If at any meeting no director is willing to act as chairman or if no director is present within 15 minutes after the time appointed for holding the meeting, the members present shall choose one of their number to be chairman of the meeting.

58.—The chairman may, with the consent of any meeting at which a quorum is present, and shall if so directed by the meeting, adjourn the meeting from time to time and from place to place, but no business shall be transacted at any adjourned meeting other than the business left unfinished at the meeting from which the adjournment took place. When a meeting is adjourned for 30 days or more, notice of the adjourned meeting shall be given as in the case of an original meeting. Save as aforesaid it shall not be necessary to give any notice of an adjournment or of the business to be transacted at an adjourned meeting.

59.—At any general meeting a resolution put to the vote of the meeting shall be decided on a show of hands unless a poll is (before or on the declaration of the result of the show of hands) demanded—

    (*a*) by the chairman; or
    (*b*) by at least three members present in person or by proxy; or
    (*c*) by any member or members present in person or by proxy and representing not less than one-tenth of the total voting rights of all the members having the right to vote at the meeting; or
    (*d*) by a member or members holding shares in the

company conferring the right to vote at the meeting being shares on which an aggregate sum has been paid up equal to not less than one-tenth of the total sum paid up on all the shares conferring that right.

Unless a poll is so demanded, a declaration by the chairman that a resolution has, on a show of hands, been carried or carried unanimously, or by a particular majority, or lost, and an entry to that effect in the book containing the minutes of the proceedings of the company shall be conclusive evidence of the fact without proof of the number or proportion of the votes recorded in favour of or against such resolution. he demand for a poll may be withdrawn.

60.—Except as provided in regulation 62, if a poll is duly demanded it shall be taken in such manner as the chairman directs, and the result of the poll shall be deemed to be the resolution of the meeting at which the poll was demanded.

61.—There is an equality of votes, whether on a show of hand or on a poll, the chairman of the meeting at which the show of hands takes place or at which the poll is demanded, shall be entitled to a second or casting vote.

62.—A poll demanded on the election of a chairman or on a question of adjournment shall be taken forthwith. A poll demanded on any other question shall be taken at such time as the chairman of the meeting directs, and any business other than that on which a poll is demanded may be proceeded with pending the taking of the poll.

Votes of Members

63.—Subject to any rights or restrictions for the time being attached to any class or classes of shares, on a show of hands every member present in person and every proxy shall have one vote, so, however, that no individual shall have more than one vote, and on a poll every member shall have one vote for each share of which he is the holder.

64.—Where there are joint holders, the vote of the senior who tenders a vote, whether in person or by proxy, shall be accepted to the exclusion of the votes of the other joint holders; and for this purpose, seniority shall be determined by the order in which the names stand in the register.

65.—A member of unsound mind, or in respect of whom an order has been made by any court having jurisdiction in lunacy, may vote, whether on a show of hands or on a poll, by his committee, receiver, guardian or other person appointed by that court and any such committee, receiver, guardian or other person may vote by proxy on a show of hands or on a poll.

66.—No member shall be entitled to vote at any general meeting unless all calls or other sums immediately payable by him in respect of shares in the company have been paid.

67.—No objection shall be raised to the qualification of any voter except at the meeting or adjourned meeting at which the vote objected to is given or tendered, and every vote not disallowed at such meeting shall be valid for all purposes. Any such objection made in due time shall be referred to the chairman of the meeting, whose decision shall be final and conclusive.

68.—Votes may be given either personally or by proxy.

69.—The instrument appointing a proxy shall be in writing under the hand of the appointer or of his attorney duly authorised in writing, or, if the appointer is a body corporate, either under seal or under the hand of an officer or attorney duly authorised. A proxy need not be a member of the company.

70.—The instrument appointing a proxy and the power of attorney or other authority, if any, under which it is signed, or a notarially certified copy of that power or authority shall be deposited at the office or at such other place within the State as is specified for that purpose in the notice convening the meeting, not less than 48 hours before the time for holding the meeting or adjourned meeting at which the person named in the instrument proposes to vote, or, in the case of a poll, not less than 48 hours before the time appointed for the taking of the poll, and, in default, the instrument of proxy shall not be treated as valid.

71.—An instrument appointing a proxy shall be in the following form or a form as near thereto as circumstances permit—

"

Limited.

I/We of .... in the County of

.... ,being a member/ members of the above-named company hereby appoint ....

....

of .... or failing

him, ...

of .... as my/our proxy to vote for me/us on my/our behalf at the (annual or extra-ordinary, as the case may be) general meeting of the company to be held on the................................... day of ...., 19...... and at any adjournment thereof.

Signed this .... day of ...., 19.......

This form is to be used as the resolution.

Unless otherwise instructed the proxy will vote as he thinks fit."

72.—The instrument appointing a proxy shall be deemed to confer authority to demand or join in demanding a poll.

73.—A vote given in accordance with the terms of an instrument of proxy shall be valid notwithstanding the previous death or insanity of the principal or revocation of the proxy or of the authority under which the proxy was executed or the transfer of the share in respect of which the proxy is given, if no intimation in writing of such death, insanity, revocation or transfer as aforesaid is received by the company at the office before the commencement of the meeting or adjourned meeting at which the proxy is used.

Bodies Corporate acting by Representatives at Meetings

74.—Any body corporate which is a member of the company may, by resolution of its directors or other governing body, authorise such person as it thinks fit to act as its representative at any meeting of the company or of any class of members of the company, and the person so authorised shall be entitled to exercise the same powers on behalf of the body corporate which he represents as that body corporate could exercise if it were an individual member of the company.

Directors

75.—The number of the directors and the names of the first directors shall be determined in writing by the subscribers of the memorandum of association or a majority of them.

76.—The remuneration of the directors shall from time to time be determined by the company in general meeting. Such remuneration shall be deemed to accrue from day to day. The directors may also be paid all travelling, hotel and other expenses properly incurred by them in attending and returning from meeting of the directors or any committee of the directors or general meetings of the company or in connection with the business of the company.

77.—The shareholding qualification for directors may be fixed by the company in general meeting and unless and until so fixed, no qualification shall be required.

78.—A director of the company may be or become a director or other officer of, or otherwise interested in, any company promoted by the company or in which the company may be interested as shareholder or otherwise, and no such director shall be accountable to the company for any remuneration or other benefits received by him as a director or officer of, or from his interest in, such other company unless the company otherwise directs.

Borrowing Powers

79.—The directors may exercise all the powers of the company to borrow money, and to mortgage or charge its undertaking, property and uncalled capital, or any part thereof, and to issue debentures, debenture stock and other securities, whether outright or as security for any debt, liability or obligation of the company or of any third party, so, however, that the amount for the time being remaining undischarged of moneys borrowed or secured by the directors as aforesaid (apart from temporary loans obtained from the company's bankers in the ordinary course of business) shall not at any time, without the previous sanction of the company in general meeting, exceed the nominal amount of the share capital of the company for the time being issued, but nevertheless no lender or other person dealing with the company shall be concerned to see or inquire whether this limit is observed. No debt incurred or security given in excess of such limit shall be invalid or ineffectual except in the case of express notice to the lender or the recipient of the security at the time when the debt was incurred or security given that the limit hereby imposed had been or was thereby exceeded.

Powers and Duties of Directors

80.—The business of the company shall be managed by the directors, who may pay all expenses incurred in promoting and registering the company and may exercise all such powers of the company as are not, by the Act or by these regulations, required to be exercised by the company in general meeting, subject, nevertheless, to any of these regulations, to the provisions of the Act and to such directions, being not inconsistent with the aforesaid regulations or provisions, as may be given by the company in general meeting; but no direction given by the company in general meeting shall invalidate any prior act of the directors which would have been valid if that direction had not been given.

81.—The directors may from time to time and at any time by power of attorney appoint any company, firm or person or body of persons, whether nominated directly or indirectly by the directors, to be the attorney or attorneys of the company for such purposes and with such powers, authorities and discretions (not exceeding those vested in or exercisable by the directors under these regulations) and for such period and subject to such conditions as they may think fit, and any such power of attorney may contain such provisions for the protection of persons dealing with any such attorney as the directors may think fit, and may also authorise any such attorney to delegate all or any of the powers, authorities and discretions vested in him.

82.—The company may exercise the powers conferred by section 41 of the Act with regard to having an official seal for use abroad, and such powers shall be vested in the directors.

83.—A director who is in any way, whether directly or

indirectly, interested in a contract or proposed contract with the company shall declare the nature of his interest at a meeting of the directors in accordance with section 194 of the Act.

84.—A director shall not vote in respect of any contract or arrangement in which he is so interested, and if he shall so vote, his vote shall not be counted, nor shall he be counted in the quorum present at the meeting but neither of these prohibitions shall apply to—

- (*a*) any arrangement for giving any director any security or indemnity in respect of money lent by him to or obligations undertaken by him for the benefit of the company; or
- (*b*) any arrangement for the giving by the company of any security to a third party in respect of a debt or obligation of the company for which the director himself has assumed responsibility in whole or in part under a guarantee or indemnity or by the deposit of a security; or
- (*c*) any contract by a director to subscribe for or under-write shares or debentures of the company; or
- (*d*) any contract or arrangement with any other company in which he is interested only as an officer of such other company or as a holder of shares or other securities in such other company;
- (*e*) these prohibitions may at any time be suspended or relaxed to any extent and either generally or in respect of any particular contract, arrangement or transaction by the company in general meeting.

85.—A director may hold any other office or place of profit under the company (other than the office of auditor) in conjunction with his office of director for such period and on such terms as to remuneration and otherwise as the directors may determine, and no director or intending director shall be disqualified by his office from contracting with the company either with regard to his tenure of any such other office or place of profit or as vendor, purchaser or otherwise, nor shall any such contract or any contract or arrangement entered into by or on behalf of the company in which any director is in any way interested, be liable to he avoided, nor shall any director so contracting or being so interested be liable to account to the company for any profit realised by any such contract or arrangement by reason of such director holding that office or of the fiduciary relation thereby established.

86.—A director, notwithstanding his interest, may be counted in the quorum present at any meeting whereat he or any other director is appointed to hold any such office or place of profit under the company or whereat the terms of any such appointment are arranged, and he may vote on any such appointment or arrangement other than his own appointment or the arrangement of the terms thereof.

87.—Any director may act by himself or his firm in a professional capacity for the company, and he or his firm shall be entitled to remuneration for professional services as if he were not a director; but nothing herein contained shall authorise a director or his firm to act as auditor to the company.

88.—All cheques, promissory notes, drafts, bills of exchange and other negotiable instruments and all receipts for moneys paid to the company shall be signed, drawn, accepted, endorsed or otherwise executed, as the case may be, by such person or persons and in such manner as the directors shall from time to time by resolution determine.

89.—The directors shall cause minutes to be made in books provided for the purpose-
        (*a*) of all appointments of officers made by the directors;

(b) of the names of the directors present at each meeting of the directors and of any committee of the directors;

(c) of all resolutions and proceedings at all meetings of the company and of the directors and of committees of directors.

90.—The directors on behalf of the company may pay a gratuity or pension or allowance on retirement to any director who has held any other salaried office or place of profit with the company or to his widow or dependants, and may make contributions to any fund and pay premium for the purchase or provision of any such gratuity, pension or allowance.

Disqualification of Directors

91.—The office of director shall be vacated if the director-

(a) ceases to be a director by virtue of section 180 of the Act; or.

(b) is adjudged bankrupt in the State or in Northern Ireland or Great Britain or makes any arrangement or composition with his creditors generally; or.

(c) becomes prohibited from being a director by reason of any order made under section 184 of the Act; or.

(d) becomes of unsound mind; or.

(e) resigns his office by notice in writing to the company; or.

(f) is convicted of an indictable offence unless the directors otherwise determine; or.

(g) is for more than 6 months absent without permission of the directors from meetings of the directors held during that period.

Rotation of Directors

92.—At the first annual general meeting of the company all the directors shall retire from office, and at the annual general meeting in every subsequent year, one-third of the directors for the time being, or, if their number is not three or a multiple of three, then the number nearest one-third shall retire from office.

93.—The directors to retire in every year shall be those who have been longest in office since their last election but as between persons who became directors on the same day, those to retire shall (unless they otherwise agree among themselves) be determined by lot.

94.—A retiring director shall be eligible for re-election.

95.—The company, at the meeting at which a director retires in manner aforesaid, may fill the vacated office by electing a person thereto, and in default the retiring director shall, if offering himself for re-election, be deemed to have been re-elected, unless at such meeting it is expressly resolved not to fill such vacated office, or unless a resolution for the re-election of such director has been put to the meeting and lost.

96.—No person other than a director retiring at the meeting shall, unless recommended by the directors, be eligible for election to the office of director at any general meeting unless not less than 3 nor more than 21 days before the day appointed for the meeting there shall have been left at the office notice in writing signed by a member duly qualified to attend and vote at the meeting for which such notice is given, of his intention to propose such person for election and also notice in writing signed by that person of his willingness to be elected.

97.—The company may from time to time by ordinary resolution increase or reduce the number of directors and may also determine in what rotation the increased or reduced number is to go out of office.

98.—The directors shall have power at any time and from time to time to appoint any person to be a director, either to fill a casual vacancy or as an addition to the existing directors, but so that the total number of directors shall not at any time exceed the number fixed in accordance with these regulations. Any director so appointed shall hold office only until the next following annual general meeting, and shall then be eligible for re-election but shall not be taken into account in determining the directors who are to retire by rotation at such meeting.

90.—The company may, by ordinary resolution, of which extended notice has been given in accordance with section 142 of the Act, remove any director before the expiration of his period of office notwithstanding anything in these regulations or in any agreement between the company and such director. Such removal shall be without prejudice to any claim such director may have for damages for breach of any contract of service between him and the company.

100.—The company may, by ordinary resolution, appoint another person in place of a director removed from office under regulation 99 and without prejudice to the powers of the directors under regulation 98 the company in general meeting may appoint any person to be a director either to fill a casual vacancy or as an additional director. A person appointed in place of a director so removed or to fill such a vacancy shall be subject to retirement at the same time as if he had become a director on the day on which the director in whose place he is appointed was last elected a director.

Proceedings of Directors
101.—The directors may meet together for the despatch of business, adjourn and otherwise regulate their meetings as they think fit. Questions arising at any meeting shall be decided by a majority of votes. Where there is an equality of votes, the chairman shall have a second or casting vote. A

director may, and the secretary on the requisition of a director shall, at any time summon a meeting of the directors. If the directors so resolve, it shall not be necessary to give notice of a meeting of directors to any director who, being resident in the State, is for the time being absent from the State.

102.—The quorum necessary for the transaction of the business of the directors may be fixed by the directors, and unless so fixed shall be two.

103.—The continuing directors may act notwithstanding any vacancy in their number but, if and so long as their number is reduced below the number fixed by or pursuant to the regulations of the company as the necessary quorum of directors, the continuing directors or director may act for the purpose of increasing the number of directors to that number or of summoning a general meeting of the company but for no other purpose.

104.—The directors may elect a chairman of their meetings and determine the period for which he is to hold office, but if no such chairman is elected, or, if at any meeting the chairman is not present within 5 minutes after the time appointed for holding the same, the directors present may choose one of their number to be chairman of the meeting.

105.—The directors may delegate any of their powers to committees consisting of such member or members of the board as they think fit; any committee so formed shall, in the exercise of the powers so delegated, conform to any regulations that may be imposed on it by the directors.

106.—A committee may elect a chairman of its meetings; if no such chairman is elected, or if at any meeting the chairman is not present within 5 minutes after the time appointed for holding the same, the members present may choose one of their number to be chairman of the meeting.

107.—A committee may meet and adjourn as it thinks proper. Questions arising at any meeting shall be determined by a majority of votes of the members present, and where there is an equality of votes, the chairman shall have a second or casting vote.

108.—All acts done by any meeting of the directors or of a committee of directors or by any person acting as a director shall, notwithstanding that it be afterwards discovered that there was some defect in the appointment of any such director or person acting as aforesaid, or that they or any of them were disqualified, be as valid as if every such person had been duly appointed and was qualified to be a director.

109.—A resolution in writing signed by all the directors for the time being entitled to receive notice of a meeting of the directors shall be as valid as if it had been passed at a meeting of the directors duly convened and held.

Managing Director

110.—The directors may from time to time appoint one or more of themselves to the office of managing director for such period and on such terms as to remuneration and otherwise as they see fit, and, subject to the terms of any agreement entered into in any particular case, may revoke such appointment. A director so appointed shall not, whilst holding that office, be subject to retirement by rotation or be taken into account in determining the rotation of retirement of directors but (without prejudice to any claim he may have for damages for breach of any contract of service between him and the company), his appointment shall be automatically determined if he ceases from any cause to be a director.

111.—A managing director shall receive such remuneration whether by way of salary, commission or participation in the profits, or partly in one way and partly in another, as the directors may determine.

112.—The directors may entrust to and confer upon a managing director any of the powers exercisable by them upon such terms and conditions and with such restrictions as they may think fit, and either collaterally with or to the exclusion of their own powers, and may from time to time revoke, withdraw, alter or vary all or any of such powers.

Secretary

113.—The secretary shall be appointed by the directors for such term, at such remuneration and upon such conditions as they may think fit; and any secretary so appointed may be removed by them.

114.—A provision of the Act or these regulations requiring or authorising a thing to be done by or to a director and the secretary shall not be satisfied by its being done by or to the same person acting both as director and as, or in place of, the secretary.

The Seal

115.—The seal shall be used only by the authority of the directors or of a committee of directors authorised by the directors in that behalf, and every instrument to which the seal shall be affixed shall be signed by a director and shall be countersigned by the secretary or by a second director or by some other person appointed by the directors for the purpose.

Dividends and Reserve

116.—The company in general meeting may declare dividends, but no dividend shall exceed the amount recommended by the directors.

117.—The directors may from time to time pay to the members such interim dividends as appear to the directors to be justified by the profits of the company.

118.—No dividend shall be paid otherwise than out of profits.

119.—The directors may, before recommending any dividend, set aside out of the profits of the company such sums as they think proper as a reserve or reserves which shall, at the discretion of the directors, be applicable for any purpose to which the profits of the company may be properly applied, and pending such application may, at the like discretion, either be employed in the business of the company or be invested in such investments as the directors may lawfully determine. The directors may also, without placing the same to reserve, carry forward any profits which they way think it prudent not to divide.

120.—Subject to the rights of persons, if any, entitled to shares with special rights as to dividend, all dividends shall be declared and paid according to the amounts paid or credited as paid on the shares in respect whereof the dividend is paid, but no amount paid or credited as paid on a share in advance of calls shall be treated for the purposes of this regulation as paid on the share. All dividends shall be apportioned and paid proportionately to the amounts paid or credited as paid on the shares during any portion or portions of the period in respect of which the dividend is paid; but if any share is issued on term providing that it shall rank for dividend as from a particular date, such share shall rank for dividend accordingly.

121.—The directors may deduct from any dividend payable to any member all sums of money (if any) immediately payable by him to the company on account of calls or otherwise in relation to the shares of the company.

122.—Any general meeting declaring a dividend or bonus may direct payment of such dividend or bonus wholly or partly by the distribution of specific assets and in particular of paid up shares, debentures or debenture stock of any other company or in any one or more of such ways, and the directors shall give effect to such resolution, and where any difficulty arises in regard to such distribution, the directors may settle the same as they think expedient, and in particular may issue fractional certificates and fix the value for distribution of such specific assets or any part thereof and may determine that cash payments shall be made to any members upon the footing of the value so fixed, in order to adjust the rights of all the parties, and may vest any such specific assets in trustees as may seem expedient to the directors.

123.—Any dividend, interest or other moneys payable in cash in respect of any shares may be paid by cheque or warrant sent through the post directed to the registered address of the holder, or, where there are joint holders, to the registered address of that one of the joint holders who is first named on the register or to such person and to such address as the holder or joint holders may in writing direct. Every such cheque or warrant shall be made payable to the order of the person to whom it is sent. Any one of two or more joint holders may give effectual receipts for any dividends, bonuses or other moneys payable in respect of the shares held by them as joint holders.

124.—No dividend shall bear interest against the company.

Accounts
125.—The directors shall cause proper books of account to be kept relating to-

      (*a*) all sums of money received and expended by the company and the matters in respect of which the receipt and expenditure takes place; and.

      (*b*) all sales and purchases of goods by the company; and.

      (*c*) the assets and liabilities of the company.

Proper books shall not be deemed to be kept if there are not kept such books of account as are necessary to give a true

and fair view of the state of the company's affairs and to explain its transactions.

126.—The books of account shall be kept at the office or, subject to section 147 of the Act, at such other place as the directors think fit, and shall at all reasonable times be open to the inspection of the directors.

127.—The directors shall from time to time determine whether and to what extent and at what times and places and under what conditions or regulations the accounts and books of the company or any of them shall be open to the inspection of members, not being directors, and no member (not being a director) shall have any right of inspecting any account or book or document of the company except as conferred by statute or authorised by the directors or by the company in general meeting.

128.—The directors shall from time to time, in accordance with sections 148, 150, 157 and 158 of the Act cause to be prepared and to be laid before the annual general meeting of the company such profit and loss accounts, balance sheets, group accounts and reports as are required by those sections to be prepared and laid before the annual general meeting of the company.

129.—A copy of every balance sheet (including every document required by law to be annexed thereto) which is to be laid before the annual general meeting of the company together with a copy of the directors' report and auditors' report shall, not less than 21 days before the date of the annual general meeting be sent to every person entitled under the provisions of the Act to receive them.

Capitalisation of Profits
130.—The company in general meeting may upon the recommendation of the directors resolve that any sum for

the time being standing to the credit of any of the company's reserves (including any capital redemption reserve fund or share premium account) or to the credit of profit and loss account be capitalised and applied on behalf of the members who would have been entitled to receive the same if the same had been distributed by way of dividend and in the same proportions either in or towards paying up amounts for the time being unpaid on any shares held by them respectively or in paying up in full unissued shares or debentures of the company of a nominal amount equal to the sum capitalised (such shares or debentures to be allotted and distributed credited as fully paid up to and amongst such holders in the proportions aforesaid) or partly in one way and partly in another, so however, that the only purpose for which sums standing to the credit of the capital redemption reserve fund or the share premium account shall be applied shall be those permitted by sections 62 and 64 of the Act.

131.—Whenever such a resolution as aforesaid shall have been passed, the directors shall make all appropriations and applications of the undivided profits resolved to be capitalised thereby and all allotments and issues of fully paid shares or debentures, if any, and generally shall do all acts and things required to give effect thereto with full power to the directors to make such provision as they shall think fit for the case of shares or debentures becoming distributable in fractions (and, in particular, without prejudice to the generality of the foregoing, to sell the shares or debentures represented by such fractions and distribute the net proceeds of such sale amongst the members otherwise entitled to such fractions in due proportions) and also to authorise any person to enter on behalf of all the members concerned into an agreement with the company providing for the allotment to them respectively credited as fully paid up of any further shares or debentures to which they may become entitled on such capitalisation or, as the case may require, for the payment up by the application thereto of their respective proportions of the profits resolved to be capitalised of the amounts remaining unpaid on their existing shares and any agreement made under such authority shall be effective and binding on all such members.

Audit

132.—Auditors shall be appointed and their duties regulated in accordance with sections 160 to 163 of the Act.

Notices

133.—A notice may be given by the company to any member either personally or by sending it by post to him to his registered address. Where a notice is sent by post, service of the notice shall be deemed to be effected by properly addressing, prepaying and posting a letter containing the notice, and to have been effected in the case of the notice of a meeting at the expiration of 24 hours after the letter containing the same is posted, and in any other case at the time at which the letter would be delivered in the ordinary course of post.

134.—A notice may be given by the company to the joint holders of a share by giving the notice to the joint holder first named in the register in respect of the share.

135.—A notice may be given by the company to the persons entitled to a share in consequence of the death or bankruptcy of a member by sending it through the post in a prepaid letter addressed to them by name or by the title of representatives of the deceased or Official Assignee in bankruptcy or by any like description at the address supplied for the purpose by the persons claiming to be so entitled, or (until such an address has been so supplied) by giving the notice in any manner in which the same might have been given if the death or bankruptcy had not occurred.

136.—Notice of every general meeting shall be given in any manner hereinbefore authorised to—

(*a*) every member; and

(*b*) every person upon whom the ownership of a share devolves by reason of his being a personal representative or the Official Assignee in bankruptcy of a member, where the member but for his death or bankruptcy would be entitled to receive notice of the meeting; and.

(*c*) the auditor for, the time being of the company.

No other person shall be entitled to receive notices of general meetings.

Winding Up

137.—If the company is wound up, the liquidator may, with the sanction of a special resolution of the company and any other sanction required by the Act, divide among the members in specie or kind the whole or any part of the assets of the company (whether they shall consist of property of the same kind or not) and may, for such purpose, set such value as he deems fair upon any property to be divided as aforesaid and may determine how such division shall be carried out as between the members or different classes of members. The liquidator may, with the like sanction, vest the whole or any part of such assets in trustees upon such trusts for the benefit of the contributories as the liquidator, with the like sanction, shall think fit, but so that no member shall be compelled to accept any shares or other securities whereon there is any liability.

Indemnity

138.—Every director, managing director, agent, auditor, secretary and other officer for the time being of the company shall be indemnified out of the assets of the company against any liability incurred by him in defending any proceedings, whether civil or criminal, in relation to his acts while acting in such office, in which judgement is given in his favour or in which he is acquitted or in connection with any application under section 391 of the Act in which relief is granted to him by the court.

Part II

Regulations for the Management of a Private Company Limited by Shares

1.—The regulations contained in Part I of Table A (with the exception of regulations 24, 51, 54, 84 and 86) shall apply.

2.—The company is a private company and accordingly—
- (*a*) the right to transfer shares is restricted in the manner hereinafter prescribed;
- (*b*) the number of members of the company (exclusive of persons who are in the employment of the company and of persons who, having been formerly in the employment of the company, were while in such employment, and have continued after the determination of such employment to be, members of the company) is limited to fifty, so, however, that where two or more persons hold one or more shares in the company jointly, they shall, for the purpose of this regulation, be treated as a single member;
- (*c*) any invitation to the public to subscribe for any shares or debentures of the company is prohibited;
- (*d*) the company shall not have power to issue share warrants to bearer.

3.—The directors may, in their absolute discretion, and without assigning any reason therefore, decline to register any transfer of any share, whether or not it is a fully paid share.

4.—Subject to sections 133 and 141 of the Act, an annual general meeting and a meeting called for the passing of a special resolution shall be called by 21 days' notice in writing at the least and a meeting of the company (other than an annual general meeting or a meeting for the passing of a special resolution) shall be called by 7 days' notice in writing at the least. The notice shall be exclusive of the day on which it is served or deemed to be served and of the day for which it is given and shall specify the day, the place and the hour of the meeting and, in the case of special business, the general nature of that business and shall be given in manner authorised by these regulations to such persons as are under the regulations of the company entitled to receive such notices from the company.

5.—No business shall be transacted at any general meeting unless a quorum of members is present at the time when the meeting proceeds to business; save as herein otherwise provided, two members present in person or by proxy shall be a quorum.

6.—Subject to section 141 of the Act, a resolution in writing signed by all the members for the time being entitled to attend and vote on such resolution at a general meeting (or being bodies corporate by their duly authorised representatives) shall be as valid and effective for all purposes as if the resolution had been passed at a general meeting of the company duly convened and held, and if described as a special resolution shall be deemed to be a special resolution within the meaning of the Act.

7.—A director may vote in respect of any contract, appointment or arrangement in which he is interested, and he shall be counted in the quorum present at the meeting.

8.—The directors may exercise the voting powers conferred by the shares of any other company held or owned by the company in such manner in all respects as they think fit and in particular they may exercise the voting powers in favour of any resolution appointing the directors or any of them as directors or officers of such other company or providing for the payment of remuneration or pensions to the directors or officers of such other company. Any director of the company may vote in favour of the exercise of such voting rights, notwithstanding that he may be or may be about to become a director or officer of such other company, and as such or in any other manner is or may be interested in the exercise of such voting rights in manner aforesaid.

9.—Any director may from time to time appoint any person who is approved by the majority of the directors to be an alternate or substitute director. The appointee, while he holds office as an alternate director, shall be entitled to notice of meetings of the directors and to attend and vote thereat as a director and shall not be entitled to be remunerated otherwise than out of the remuneration of the director appointing him. Any appointment under this regulation shall be effected by notice in writing given by the appointer to the secretary. Any appointment so made may be revoked at any time by the appointer or by a majority of the other directors or by the company in general meeting. Revocation by an appointer shall be effected by notice in writing given by the appointer to the secretary.

Note—Regulations 3, 4 and 5 of this Part are alternative to regulations 24, 51 and 54 respectively of Part I. Regulations 7 and 8 of this Part are alternative to regulations 84 and 86 of Part 1.

Memorandum of Association

TABLE B

FORM OF MEMORANDUM OF ASSOCIATION OF A COMPANY LIMITED BY SHARES

1.—The name of the company is "The Western Mining Company, Limited".

2.—The objects for which the company is established are the mining of minerals of all kinds and the doing of all such other things as are incidental or conducive to the attainment of the above object.

3.—The liability of the members is limited.

4.—The share capital of the company is £200,000, divided into 200,000 shares of £1 each.

We, the several persons whose names and addresses are subscribed, wish to be formed into a company in pursuance of this memorandum of association, and we agree to take the number of shares in the capital of the company set opposite our respective names.

Names, Addresses and Descriptions of Subscribers	Number of Shares taken by each Subscriber
1. James Walsh of .... in the County of .... Solicitor	50
2. John Murphy of .... in the County of .... Engineer	2,700
3. Patrick Ryan of .... in the County of .... Geologist	1,250
4. Thomas O'Connell of .... in the County of .... Engineer	500
5. Daniel Clarke of .... in the County of .... Geologist	50
6. Patrick Byrne of .... in the County of .... Accountant	300
7. John Collins of .... in the County of .... Solicitor	150
Total Shares taken	5,000

Dated the......................day of...................... 19............

Witness to the above Signatures:

Name: ....

Address: ....

....

....

Index